REA **ACPL ITEM**

3 1833 05

DISC

||||||||||||||||||||||||||||||
D0130841

THE BLUEST STATE

THE BLUEST STATE

*How Democrats Created the
Massachusetts Blueprint for
American Political Disaster*

JON KELLER

St. Martin's Press 𝄞 New York

www.stmartins.com

Library of Congress Cataloging-in-Publication Data

Keller, Jon (Jon Peter)
   The bluest state : how democrats created the Massachusetts blueprint for American political disaster / Jon Keller. — 1st ed.
       p.   cm.
   ISBN-13: 978-0-312-36831-9
   ISBN-10: 0-312-36831-3
   1. Massachusetts—Politics and government—1951–
2. Political culture—Massachusetts.   3. Political corruption—Massachusetts.   4. Massachusetts—Social conditions.
5. United States—Politics and government—1989–
6. Political culture—United States.   7. Political corruption—United States.   8. Liberalism—United States.   9. Democratic Party (U. S.)   10. Baby boom generation—United States—Political activity.   I. Title.

F71. K45   2007
306.209744—dc22   2007019468

First Edition: September 2007

10   9   8   7   6   5   4   3   2   1

For Inez, who chases my blues away

CONTENTS

....

ACKNOWLEDGMENTS

··

The Bluest State would not have been written without the initiative and wise counsel of Eve Bridburg, a thoughtful and talented agent with Zachary Shuster Harmsworth and a Boston literary guru through her work with the Grub Street independent creative writing center. Along with Esmond Harmsworth, Eve provided invaluable support every step of the way, and I'm grateful for having had her in my corner. Thanks also to my editor, Michael Flamini, for his enthusiasm and creative spark.

The Bluest State is a by-product of twenty-nine years of close contact with Massachusetts politics in a variety of roles, including radio news reporter, producer, and talk-show host; newspaper reporter, editor, and columnist; magazine writer; and television analyst, reporter, and interviewer. At every step of the way, nurturing managers and editors set me loose, reined me in, and taught me the ropes. In roughly chronological order, my warmest thanks to Gail Jennes, Bob Fish, Steve Mindich, Mark Jurkowitz, Peter Kadzis, Jack Fitzgerald, Ron Becker, Peter Temple, Dan Fickes, Dave Gwizdowski, George Vago, Greg Caputo, Pam Johnston, John Vitanovec, Vinny Manzi, Diane D'Ercole, Theresa Moore, Kathy McSweeney,

Brian Sullivan, Steve Carro, Pat Durkin, Randy Murdoch, Ellen Clegg, David Greenway, Herb Lipson, Dan Scully, John Strahinich, Jon Marcus, James Burnett, Pat Purcell, Joe Sciacca, Marty Peretz, and John Fund.

Most journalists are lucky to have one mentor; I've been blessed with two who played an important role in my journalistic and personal development. Russel Pergament, the Tab Newspapers publisher who gave me my first column, not only provided unflagging encouragement, but also taught me a crucial lesson: politicians are not gods, they're people, and to earn their respect and attention, an occasional sharp elbow upside the head may be required. And the late David Brudnoy, my partner in radio talk-show crime for six years, became my role model in work ethic and independent thought, my biggest booster, and my surrogate big brother. My unending gratitude to both of them.

During the writing of *The Bluest State*, I was extremely fortunate to have ever-supportive day-job bosses: Ed Piette, Angie Kucharski, Jennifer Street, Tim White, David Hatcher, and David Kaplar at WBZ-TV, and Ted Jordan and Peter Casey at WBZ Radio. Thanks also to friends outside the office, including Barbara and Charley Manning, Howie Carr, William Schneider, and Michael Barone. Profound gratitude to Cary Pahigian, my friend and counselor for thirty years. My pal and colleague Steve Freyer has been an indispensable source of good advice and positive energy. Ditto Nancy Palmer, Dick Gross, Jill Mesirov, Eliza Blanchard, Ralph Child, Tina Hansar, Karl Laubscher, Sue Post, Woody Lichtenstein, Kevin Myron, Peter Meade, Ward Cromer, and Fred Burnham. A special thanks to

Jim Mintz and Deborah Stewart for their important early encouragement.

Morton Keller, a distinguished American historian, and Phyllis Keller, a legendary academic administrator, provided essential feedback along the way. But then again, as the best parents any blue-state boy could ever want, perhaps they're to blame for the whole project. Love and thanks also to my sister, Robin Keller, for her advice and enthusiasm, and to my ever supportive in-laws, Brian Cogan, Ruth and Steve Sherman, and Jamie Larowitz. My beloved sons, Barney and Jared, contributed more to this book than they know; every time my energy flagged, I thought of the possibility that my admonitions for change might somehow help them find a future close by me here in Massachusetts, and I was inspired to get back to work.

And to my wife, Inez, "thank you" seems completely inadequate. Without your love and inspiration, there would be no me.

Jon Keller

THE BLUEST STATE

Introduction

INCREDIBLY, IT'S HAPPENING again.

A presidential campaign is underway with a Massachusetts politician cast in a key role. Can the show ever go on without one? Three of the last ten Democratic presidential nominees were from here: John F. Kennedy in 1960, Michael Dukakis in 1988, and John Kerry in 2004. Massachusetts also launched two failed but buzz-generating candidacies, Ted Kennedy in 1980 and the late Sen. Paul Tsongas in 1992. All told, four of the last seven presidential elections have had a Massachusetts horse in the field. Only Texas has produced more candidates during that time.

Have you ever wondered why America's thirteenth-largest state casts such a large shadow on our national politics? You may think you know Massachusetts. Maybe you went to college or graduate school here, courting your future spouse in the funky coffee shops and left-wing bookstores of Cambridge or Amherst.

Perhaps you dragged the family on a history buff's holiday, immersing yourselves in the cobblestoned legacy that is a key source of our outsized self-esteem. And even if you've never made the pilgrimage to the Kennedy Library, taken the bus tour of JFK's old Boston haunts, or driven by the Hyannisport compound where so much modern history has been made, you surely know of our role as the birthplace of the most powerful liberal legend of our times, and as the keepers of its modern-day flame.

But this time around, there's a twist to the traditional Massachusetts influence. Instead of the usual liberal Democrat, Massachusetts's gift to the body politic is a Republican, former Gov. Mitt Romney, who has proven to be a mixed blessing. He exudes the entitled air that often accompanies the fabulously rich and handsome on their rounds. For moderate Republicans and right-leaning independents, Romney's staunch social conservatism is off-putting; to true right-wingers, his self-serving "evolution" on issues such as abortion rights, stem-cell research, and gay marriage smacks of flagrant political opportunism. Justifiably, some wonder: can the GOP hold the White House in 2008 with a candidate who is both dogmatic and expedient?

The opposition might well ask themselves the same question. With Bush fatigue on the march, the time couldn't be better for Democrats to secure the control over the courts, the economy, and U.S. foreign policy that they've craved for nearly three decades, absent that brief bout of Clintonus interruptus. And for boomer liberals who've been waiting for an extended shot at realizing the political lives they've always imagined, it's a make-or-break moment, with failure likely to usher in a regret-laden retirement.

But with even the youngest boomers now past forty, generational self-doubt still lingers. The youthful dreams so many
of us had of one day taking undisputed charge and bringing a
visionary new style of politics to a grateful nation are deteriorating right along with our eyesight and hairlines. Consider the
presidential nominees the liberal wing of our generation has
produced so far: John Kerry (born 1943); Bill Clinton (1946);
Al Gore (1948). Ambitious, one and all. Intelligent to varying
degrees. Each was in one way or another brought low by gen-
erationally recognizable flaws: corrosive narcissism, overweening self-confidence, unbridled unctuousness. None is likely to
be remembered by historians in a class with the great politicians of generations past. (Attention, Republicans: don't forget
the forgettable likes of Dan Quayle [1947], Newt Gingrich
[1943], and George W. Bush [1946].)

Is there an idealistic boomer Democrat anywhere in America
who is satisfied with the tenuous recovery of House and Senate
majorities in 2006? Perhaps Hillary Clinton (1947) or a late-wave
upstart like Barack Obama (1961) will break the boomer pattern
of demoralizing defeat and squandered opportunity come 2008.
Or maybe boomer liberals will follow the story line they began in
1972 with George McGovern, only to find themselves in late
middle age wrestling with a bad dose of writer's block.

Which brings us back to Massachusetts, where so much of
that script has been written, and to Romney, who early on in
his political career told a profound truth about the brand of
boomer liberalism that dominates the nation's bluest state.

In the fall of 1994, Ted Kennedy was in political trouble.
Massachusetts was not sharing in the nation's economic recovery,

and the natives were restless. Ted's approval rating was down after a bad run of publicity about his boozy social habits. A late-summer poll found Romney, a fresh-faced venture capitalist, running even with the last Kennedy brother.

In a political environment created by and infused with the Kennedy legend, this was unthinkable. No Kennedy had ever lost an election in Massachusetts. After Labor Day, an alarmed Ted turned up the juice. He brought in a seasoned political pro to replace his inept boomer nephew, Michael Kennedy, as campaign manager. He unleashed another nephew, Congressman Joe Kennedy, to remind voters in this heavily Catholic state of Romney's Mormon faith and to spread outdated gossip about the Mormon church's segregationist practices. Ted poured millions into TV ads trashing Romney as a corporate vulture. Ted pulled his personal act together as well, sharpening his stump speech and dispelling doubts about his competence with a sharp performance in the first of two mid-October TV debates. Postdebate polls for the first time showed a comfortable double-digit Kennedy lead.

Still, the Kennedy campaign wasn't taking any chances. The final debate was a classic political setup. Kennedy insisted on staging the event at Holyoke Community College, located in a true-blue corner of western Massachusetts, where the local papers don't often dwell on Kennedy family foibles and the college president was an old political ally. Questions came from a "citizen panel" stacked with Kennedy sycophants, lobbing softballs designed to accentuate the incumbent's long history of delivering federal funds to the state. Romney desperately needed to engage Kennedy directly, but the format didn't allow it.

With time running out in the statewide broadcast, a frustrated Romney used his closing statement to go for the jugular. He looked directly into the camera, his normally sunny expression contorted into an angry stare.

"I was in Dorchester not long ago," he said, referring to an especially rundown section of a sprawling Boston neighborhood that includes, in one of its nicer precincts, the John F. Kennedy Presidential Library and Museum. "Someone said, 'This is Kennedy country,' and they handed a sign to me in front of my face," Romney continued. "And I looked around and I saw boarded-up buildings, and I saw jobs leaving, and I said, 'It looks like it.'"

Kennedy country. The crowd gasped. Bad enough that Romney had dared run against a Kennedy and made him sweat. Now he was bluntly deriding the core political identity of not just the Kennedy family, but an entire generation of Democrats as well. *Kennedy country.* Uttered with the same unvarnished contempt a Massachusetts Democrat would typically reserve for references to Ronald Reagan or George W. Bush.

Sitting in their hard-to-heat living rooms in hard-to-afford homes across Massachusetts, watching the debate on TV, scores of beleaguered working-class people were no doubt startled, too. In this overwhelmingly one-party state, folks aren't used to hearing Democratic mythology questioned in public. But once in a great while in politics an unexpected moment of truth breaks through the conventional wisdom erected to keep honesty at bay. Security is breached, allowing an unwelcome fact to slip in and dash across the playing field, startling the crowd and embarrassing the swells in the luxury boxes. This was one of those moments, especially shocking because it happened in Massachusetts, home to one of the nation's most uniform, carefully policed political cultures.

Kennedy country: in theory, full of working-class neighborhoods endowed with equal rights and opportunity courtesy of an enlightened, activist government. America made livable for all. That's the vision so many boomers inherited from the Kennedy family. A previous generation had created a New Deal out of crisis and pragmatism. Now their descendants, spared the character-building experiences of economic depression and world war and suffused with personal idealism, would stake out "new frontiers" for New Deal precepts. This "new generation of Americans" was "unwilling to witness or permit the slow undoing of . . . human rights," John Kennedy declared in his 1961 inaugural address. "The future does not belong to those who are content with today, apathetic toward common problems and their fellow man alike, timid and fearful in the face of bold projects and new ideas," preached Bobby Kennedy a few years later. "It will belong to those who can blend passion, reason and courage in a personal commitment to the great enterprises and ideals of American society." The last Kennedy brother renewed this generational mandate in his 1980 Democratic Convention speech: "The work goes on, the cause endures, the hope still lives, and the dream shall never die."

To millions of Americans who grew up on the stories of the Kennedys, the civil rights movement, the Vietnam War, and Watergate, these words still have profound meaning. Their inspirational rhythms connect with many boomers like a still-beloved guitar solo from a long-ago classic hit. And especially for Massachusetts liberals of this generation, it's not just a gauzy memory. Massachusetts is full of schools, libraries, and bus tours that trade on the Kennedy name. But it's much more than an animatronic theme park. This is the homeland of New Frontier Politics 3.0, of boomer liberals all grown up and calling the shots. It's a working laboratory for their policies and a training camp for many of the activists and candidates who have defined the Democratic Party since the 1960s. To them, it's been a big success—their love of self-congratulation would allow no other conclusion. And they didn't appreciate the sight of a midwestern Mormon, a corporate takeover artist with a car salesman's patter and impossibly perfect hair, getting in their faces and crying fraud.

Mitt Romney had entered the den of American liberalism and urinated on the shag carpet by singling out the defining symbol of an entire political culture's self-esteem and pronouncing it a failure. In the testosterone-fueled world of Massachusetts politics, turning the other cheek usually describes a hostile act of rear-end exposure, and the Democratic establishment was livid. The next day, at a rally for Ted Kennedy in Dorchester's Adams Corner commercial district, a parade of top Democrats excoriated Romney as a "cheap shot" artist. Friendly editorialists expressed horror. "If Dorchester were a bride, she would be offended by such a misogynistic remark," sniffed one. Ted himself, comforted by the polls, was dismissive. "We will board up Mitt Romney and put him out of business," he roared. "What did you expect from somebody from Grosse Pointe, Michigan?"

Kennedy won reelection by a double-digit margin. But eight years later, Romney ran again, this time for governor of Massachusetts. The race matched a conservative Mormon male

against a relatively moderate liberal (by Massachusetts standards), Democrat Shannon O'Brien, the state's first-ever female
gubernatorial nominee. As he had in the run against Kennedy
eight years earlier, Romney stressed the state's economic and social decay during years of near-total Democratic control. He
hammered away at the cronyism and mismanagement that had
plunged the state deep into debt and led to mammoth cost overruns on the Big Dig, the infamous downtown Boston highway
project. He mocked O'Brien for losing millions in worker pension funds on bad investments. And he linked her with unpopular leaders of the Democrat-controlled state legislature. In the
nation's bluest state, red paid off. Romney won easily, the third
straight Republican to win the governorship in a place where
Democrats held a lock on every other major political office.

Are you baffled by this strange state, where liberals rule and
Kennedys never lose, but where the same voters who paint the
state so blue sometimes revolt against their own color scheme?
Are you confused at the sight of Democrats, many of them
disguised as independents, expressing such mixed emotions
about their Kennedy country paradise? If you knew what the
working people of Massachusetts had been going through for
the past few decades, you wouldn't be.

In the pages that follow, I'll tell you something about
Kennedy country you likely don't know. Its most important
vow—of a government in touch with and devoted to the
working classes and the poor, delivering on its commitment to
improve their lives and enhance their opportunities—has
turned out to be a broken promise. This is the sorry story of
their shabby treatment at the hands of purported liberal sav-

iors, boomers who've lived up to their generation's reputation for narcissism and self-delusion, let down those who believed their lofty rhetoric of change, and injected their politically poisonous habits into the national Democratic party. As much as those on the right may enjoy the spectacle, it's also a cautionary tale for boomer conservatives who too often evince the same pathology. But while it's a warning for them, it's a DEFCON 1 alert for Democrats who can almost taste the full Washington takeover they've craved for so long. And just as Tom Frank's *What's the Matter with Kansas?* was a shout out to liberals about the way Republicans were eating their lunch in the heartland, *The Bluest State* is a reminder of how recklessly boomer liberals dig their own graves.

More than a decade after Mitt Romney gave his caustic take on the Kennedy legacy, the North Dorchester neighborhood where he was heckled by Kennedy partisans is still plagued by abandoned buildings and joblessness. Drug abuse and its criminal side effects are rampant. After rave reviews for Boston's anticrime "miracle" programs during the 1990s, violent street crime is once again soaring in North Dorchester and other poor city neighborhoods. In Holyoke, the impoverished old mill city in the state's chronically depressed western region that hosted the Kennedy-Romney debate, more than half the children, most of them Puerto Rican immigrants, live below the poverty line. Statewide, white-collar job growth has been flat at a time of national economic recovery; good blue-collar jobs, especially in the vanishing manufacturing sector, are even scarcer. In recent years Massachusetts has twice scored an unwanted distinction: it is the only state in the nation to lose net population, as mobile residents vote with their feet on the state's sky-high cost of living, dwindling opportunities, and deteriorating quality of life.

The Democrats from Ted Kennedy on down who've had nearly total control of the state for three decades talk a big game about their vision of a better deal for the masses. But their abysmal track record tells a different tale, one made especially relevant to the future of the Democratic Party nationally by the political circumstances of the Massachusetts debacle.

Just as voters in 2006 recoiled from the results of GOP control of all three governmental branches, they may shrink in horror from the sight of what total Democratic domination produces. Uniquely among the fifty states, Massachusetts over the past few decades has been a Democrats' Burger King: they always have it their way. The only two Republicans in the ten-member Massachusetts congressional delegation were expelled in 1996. After the Romney scare, Ted Kennedy was reelected in 2000 and 2006 without serious opposition. Sen. John Kerry ran completely unopposed in 2002. An ultra-liberal Democrat, Deval Patrick, Bill Clinton's assistant attorney general for civil rights, broke the string of Republican gubernatorial victories in 2006, cementing our status as the nation's bluest state.

The Massachusetts Republican party has been a desiccated shell for years. Since 1992 the paltry GOP contingent in the state legislature hasn't had the numbers to sustain a veto by one of those Republican governors. In 2002, the state ranked behind only South Carolina in percentage of legislative seats left uncontested by a major party; in 2006 the fringe Green/Rainbow Party mounted more candidates for statewide office than the GOP. Accordingly, Massachusetts has become a national symbol of unleavened liberalism. Romney cracks rueful jokes about it when he speaks to out-of-state audiences. Being a Republican in Massachusetts, he says in a guaranteed laugh line, is like being "a cattle rancher at a vegetarian convention."

Romney's Dorchester heckler had, at least, been candid: the Kennedy country he was urging Romney to vacate is a place where meat-eaters offering any serious counterpoint to the political status quo need not apply. For more than a decade, the same Democratic leaders who rightfully decry Republican hegemony in Washington have spent every election year urging Massachusetts voters to abandon even the most token party balance. Rogue Democrats who show affection for the occasional moderate Republican are ostracized by the Democratic party and stripped of their delegate status at the state convention. Beyond party loyalty, liberal policy hegemony is enforced; moderate or conservative Democrats who dare endorse too much tax relief or balk at rubber-stamping the agenda of key Democratic special-interest groups face scathing public reprimand or exile. Massachusetts has become a Brigadoon of 1960's liberalism, where admissions of failure and openness to revisionist political thinking are rarely, if ever, seen.

From the perspective of establishment Democrats enjoying virtually unchallenged incumbency, it's a comfortable formula. While signs of serious public discontent have been evident at times in anti-tax referendum votes, pessimistic opinion poll results, and that aberrant streak of GOP governors, the Republicans, with barely thirteen percent of the registered voters behind them, rarely capitalize. Because they win here so easily and habitually, it doesn't seem to bother local Democrats when the rest of the country mocks the state as a dominion of knee-jerk, left-wing losers. "Taxachusetts," they call us. The People's Republic of Massachusetts. "The Democratic National Committee announced that it had chosen Boston as the site for the [2004] convention," joked Brookline native Conan O'Brien, a few years back. "It's a perfect match because neither the Democrats nor the Red Sox can win in the fall."

Actually, the Sox finally won one in 2004. But days after the Sox clinched in St. Louis, the Democratic Party blew a perfectly winnable presidential election. Again. With a son of Massachusetts at the helm. Again. When the political and cultural affectations of Massachusetts became an issue in the Kerry-Bush race, just as they had with Dukakis-Bush back in 1988, the locals took it as a point of pride. There go the yahoos again. What did you expect from somebody from Grosse Pointe, Michigan?

But while Massachusetts liberals relax in their blue Eden, the rest of the nation's Democrats are still reeling from their agonizing failure to finish off the credibility-impaired Bush administration in 2004. Anxious hand-wringing and soul-searching have been pouring out of the nation's liberal think tanks, college campuses, publishing houses, and op-ed pages like brackish water through a ruptured levee that even the latest round of congressional victories can't seal up. The Democrats have strayed too far from Clinton-era centrism, argue the former president's old pals from the Democratic Leadership Council (DLC), pointing to the comparatively right-leaning candidates who broke through in 2006. No, the problem is the party has drunk too much of that centrist Kool-Aid and lost its progressive souls, counter liberals like E. J. Dionne, Robert

Reich, and the fervent bloggers and posters of the netroots. Actually it's the fault of overly contrived consultants and spin doctors, claims journalist Joe Klein in *Politics Lost*. Or maybe it's just a matter of personal style undermining political righteousness. "Our economic agenda and the messaging associated with it must share the blame," claim the leaders of the Third Way project, a DLC-like collective. If only liberals didn't let the right get away with describing tax "cuts" as tax "relief," complains linguist George Lakoff. "Reframing" and "rebranding" are the verbs of the hour—quite the rhetorical climbdown from "the dream shall never die." It's all in the way you say it, these thinkers believe.

To a generation obsessed with style, *The Bluest State* argues that substance still matters. Hours before a debate in his 1996 Senate reelection fight with Bill Weld, the Republican governor of Massachusetts, aides to Sen. John Kerry pulled a host official aside. The looking glass in the senator's dressing room just won't do, they explained; he'd prefer to have his own, freestanding antique mirror brought in. Of course he would. Kerry is emblematic of a generation that likes to work up a political and moral sweat in front of a full-length mirror. But what about, for once, making an honest accounting of what the mirror shows? Not at how the contrivances of boomer liberalism look in the glass or how they parse their rhetoric, but at what they've actually done with the virtually unrestrained power they've wielded in their most exclusive political province on behalf of the people they claim to care about most?

How did historic, proudly blue Massachusetts become an easy late-night TV laugh? How did a state that once held the

New Frontier high ground of American political liberalism become a discredited backwater, a kiss-of-death address for national candidates? What caused the home of the "Hub of the Universe" to slip so badly into working-class decay that young residents would abandon its exorbitant living costs and stunted opportunities as if fleeing an onrushing tsunami? Why is this self-avowed citadel of diversity such a hostile political environment for women and black candidates, notwithstanding the unexpected 2006 election of our first African American governor? The most important ideas in our political conversation—about human rights, urban governance, education reform, and foreign policy—once flowed freely from Massachusetts. Why do they now originate elsewhere, while we make the news as a can-you-believe-this-one kicker on the late news for our foolish political and social excesses?

The answers may be hard to swallow for some. They indict the foibles of a well-meaning generation that thinks of itself as many things—thinkers, innovators, and righteous crusaders—but never as pretentious failures. Throughout an era of conservative Republican ascendancy, liberal boomers everywhere have looked to Massachusetts as a true-blue bulwark against the insidious red tide. In 1988 and 2004, Democratic pragmatists turned to Massachusetts politicians they mistakenly thought had concocted the magic antidote to Republican strengths. Michael Dukakis would embody "competence" by comparison with bumbling George H. W. Bush. War hero John Kerry would provide a stark contrast of true military strength and intelligence against Bush-the-younger's AWOL imbecility. Underlying those disastrous candidacies—still dismissed by clueless boomers as victims of clever GOP manipulation rather than deserving failures—was the hope that the healing waters of Kennedy country, so carefully and lovingly preserved at their ancestral Massachusetts home, might one day be released across America, washing away the damage done by Ronald Reagan, George W. Bush, and company, irrigating a progressive revival, and, of course, lifting all boats.

But those pipe dreams deserve filing away in the attic along with the bong, the Country Joe and the Fish records, and other musty artifacts of bygone boomer youth. Romney was right. Kennedy country is a marketing sham. It's the retro brand name for an impotent snake oil that doesn't deliver relief for the working-class people it purports to help the most.

Let me show you around my beloved but obtuse home state. It's a place where bright people with good educations and well-paying careers live within easy reach of some of America's most gorgeous seashore and countryside. We are home to the preferred vacation haunts of the nation's liberal tastemakers and intelligentsia: the Berkshires, Cape Cod, Nantucket, and Martha's Vineyard. Picnicking on the banks of the Charles River as fireworks light up the skyline and the Boston Pops perform on July Fourth, it's debatable whether there's any place in the country more handsome, historic, European.

But off the beaten tourist and vacation-home tracks lies a different Massachusetts. This other state is a place where the poor lack hope and live in Appalachia-like squalor, where even middle-class workers with salaries well above the national median struggle to afford inferior housing, hold jobs that barely subsidize survival, and wait in vain for meaningful help from the state government. Visitors enjoy the shrines to our historic profiles in courage: the minutemen, the Founding Fathers, John F. Kennedy. But the stops on their tour are never more than a few blocks away from profiles in discouragement and mismanagement, the blighted neighborhoods and stunted hopes of the state's poor and working classes. Our tangible symbols of the best in American politics—from the Freedom Trail's walk through the breeding grounds of American democracy, to the Kennedy Library's elaborate homage to modern-day Democratic liberalism—sit in the shadow of appalling symbols of governmental failure like the Big Dig, that fatally dangerous $15 billion monument to the Massachusetts political culture's greed and carelessness.

Prepare to visit the un-Camelot, where a set of customs and conceits are running loose and need to be corralled before they kill off any more boomer dreams or Democratic presidential tickets. Kennedy country and its political culture aren't good role models for Democrats anymore. They aren't even a benign throwback to a happier time. They're poison. And it's time for those boomers who truly want to, as one paean to their generation put it, "look for what is real, what is honest, what is quality, what is important," to take an honest look at how the Massachusetts model is driving American liberalism off a bridge.

CHAPTER ONE

....

What's Wrong with Massachusetts

ON THAT DARK April day in 1968 when Dr. Martin Luther King Jr. was assassinated, a boomer political icon was sanctified. Sen. Robert F. Kennedy broke the news of King's murder to a black audience in Indianapolis with a speech Joe Klein would, nearly forty years later, call "a sublime example of the substance and music of politics in its grandest form, for its highest purpose—to heal, to educate, to lead."

"For those of you . . . tempted to be filled with hatred and disgust of the injustice of such an act, against all white people, I can only say that . . . I had a member of my family killed," said Kennedy. He quoted Aeschylus on drawing wisdom from pain and closed with a plea for racial harmony. "The vast majority of white people and the vast majority of black people in this country want to live together, want to improve the quality of our life, and want justice for all human beings who abide in our land. Let us dedicate ourselves to that . . . and say a prayer for our country, and for our people."

In the carnage that followed the King assassination, hundreds of people were injured and three thousand arrested in a wave of street violence, arson, and looting of major cities. But thanks in part to the eloquence of a Kennedy, Indianapolis stayed quiet. And so did Boston, Massachusetts, thanks to the quick thinking of its own enlightened young leadership.

By coincidence, soul singer James Brown was scheduled to play the Boston Garden the night after the King assassination. The cops, fearful of any large gathering of blacks, wanted to cancel the show. But Boston's newly elected mayor, Kevin White, and Tom Atkins, the city's first black city councilor, asked the local public broadcasting station to televise the concert instead in hopes of keeping people off the streets.

This impromptu marriage of musical and political soul accomplished what, in other cities, a show of police force could not. Young black Bostonians stayed home to watch Brown perform and join Mayor White onstage to deliver a fervent appeal for calm. White, who would be on George McGovern's vice-presidential shortlist four years later, called on the audience to "make Dr. King's dream a reality for Boston. . . . No matter what any other community might do, we in Boston will honor Dr. King in peace." It was a proud new chapter in a once-fading industrial city's renaissance as the capital of the New Frontier. A minor incident in the context of that awful week, perhaps, like any good news about something that didn't happen. But for relieved and grateful Bostonians, the quick reflexes of White and Atkins were a sneak preview of how young, progressive leadership—the emerging "new genera-tion" touted by John Kennedy—might rewrite the political playbook.

These were its promises: government would no longer be the top-down province of elites, but a new, populist coalition. Grad-uates of leafy campuses like Williams (Kevin White's alma mater), Swarthmore (where future governor Michael Dukakis got his degree), and it goes without saying, Harvard and Yale, would take the wheel from an older generation of ward-heeler pols who lacked fancy diplomas. But alongside in the front seat, sharing map duty, would be organized labor, women, and mi-norities. Unrest over atrocities like the King assassination would be met not with baton-wielding police, but with rhythm and blues and its political equivalent, Kennedyesque appeals to America's better self. The apparatus of power would be made to work on behalf of the disenfranchised, with progressive prin-ciples as a guide. This was not merely a secular goal. As Bobby Kennedy put it, back when religious references in political rhet-oric were noncontroversial: "We must recognize the full human equality of all our people—before God, before the law, and in the councils of government. We must do this not because it is economically advantageous—although it is; not because the laws of God and man command it—although they do command it; not because people in other lands wish it so. We must do it for the single and fundamental reason that it is the right thing to do."

Massachusetts political leaders have held these principles as their marching orders ever since. For a generation known to be inseparable from their loving memories of personal water-sheds, it isn't surprising that the Kennedys, the first political love affairs for many boomers, retain their national mystique. But here in Kennedy country, it's more like an obsession. In local Democratic circles, if you were too young to have worked for Jack in 1960 or Bobby in 1968, you likely paid your dues with Ted's 1980 presidential or subsequent Senate runs, or the congressional campaigns of young Joe, Bobby's eldest. Absent a direct connection, boomer Massachusetts pols still mimic the style, airing TV ads showing themselves in shirtsleeves, tie loosened, rubbing elbows with a meticulously diverse array of grateful citizens. This imagery is as common a sight here as a Dunkin' Donuts drive-through, and the impact is more than just stylistic. Inspired by the confluence of Kennedy-era liberalism and its own historic activism, Massachusetts has become a prime test kitchen for the boomers' liberal impulses and political culture. We are quick to expand the notion of commonwealth, most recently defining it to include universal health coverage and full legal marriage rights for gays and lesbians. As one state senator put it during the legislative debate over same-sex marriage. "Massachusetts has always been the conscience of the nation. That is our role."

Hasn't it always been? Massachusetts men led the charge against the British and established the first major beachhead of American intellectualism at Harvard. Our best known thinkers—Emily Dickinson, Ralph Waldo Emerson, and Henry David Thoreau—still pack cachet. When Venezuelan president Hugo Chavez denounced George W. Bush as "Satan" at the UN in 2006, he brandished the latest book by MIT professor Noam Chomsky, not a tract from some two-bit Berkeley or Ann Arbor academic. We've done more than think big

thoughts. The populist foundations of American life origi-
nated here. Bostonians were the first city dwellers to ride a
public transit system to work, the first to attend public schools
and enjoy public libraries. When Ronald Reagan referred to
America as "a shining city on a hill," he was cribbing an old
nickname for Boston. Our commitment to activist government
extends back to the Mayflower Compact of 1620, when free-
thinking Pilgrims made the formation of a "civil body politic"
their first priority. It continues through John Adams, the grand-
daddy of federalism, to James Michael Curley ("the mayor of
the poor") and—lest we forget—the Kennedys. During this unmatched history of innovation and creativity, Massachusetts has
been center stage for some of America's most profound political
debates—over the rights and responsibilities of citizens in a
democracy, the immorality of slavery, the moral imperatives of
racial justice, and the definition of a just war.

Our robust self-esteem also has deep roots in the Massachusetts political culture. The first seal of the newly chartered
Massachusetts Bay Colony in the early seventeenth century featured an Indian begging the Pilgrims to "come over and help
us," a plea imagined by colonists who hadn't even set foot yet in
this allegedly needy New World. More than a century ago,
Bostonians modestly called their city the "Hub of the Universe." The boomers who run the show today, in keeping with
that generation's reputation for immodesty, see no reason to
change the nickname. "How we treat our most vulnerable,
how we provide the greatest opportunity for our citizens . . .
these are the building blocks of a foundation that was established first in Massachusetts," bragged House Speaker Sal Di-

Masi, a liberal Democrat, in his inaugural speech. "Massachusetts has been getting it right for more than 300 years."

Given the state's disproportionate importance in national Democratic and liberal circles, this hubris seems justified to those who wallow in it. For the past half-century, Massachusetts has held unmatched sway over the national Democratic Party. In addition to that extraordinary run of presidential candidates, the state has been home to two of the last five Democratic Speakers of the U.S. House. Massachusetts has been the source of an unceasing supply of top Democratic political consultants, strategists, field organizers, pollsters, and academic policy wonks. Even our backbencher congressmen are familiar national figures on the cable TV talk shows, from openly gay Rep. Barney Frank to campaign-finance-reform crusader Rep. Marty Meehan. In the Bush era, our senators and members of congress have been the front line of partisan attack.

Massachusetts's political clout is not a fluke. It has roots in the state's contemporary history as a powerful cultural and political influence on the boomers.

Growing up in Cambridge, the son of a history professor and an academic administrator, I knew I lived someplace special and influential. By the standards of late-1960s America, the experience was about as hip as a childhood could be, or so we believed. On a sunny Saturday, while Andy of Mayberry out there in flyover country had gone fishing, my teenage friends and I were on our bikes cruising around Harvard Square, pedaling through clouds of pot smoke on the Cambridge Common, watching Sly and the Family Stone play for free for the local hippies, catching the occasional whiff of tear gas left over from an antiwar demonstration.

The first wave of boomers was graduating from college and turning Massachusetts college towns into prime breeding grounds for many of the progressive politicians, policy wonks, and cultural critics who make American liberalism what it is today. Their peers in New York, Madison, Wisconsin, and San Francisco were doing their part. But Massachusetts in the 1960s was a wellspring for a counterculture celebrating rock music and experimentation with drugs. The Who and Led Zepplin first performed for American audiences at local clubs like the Boston Tea Party, and Harvard gave Timothy Leary the space he needed to get to the bottom of LSD. At the turn of the decade, as resistance to the "Amerikkkan war machine" came into vogue, Massachusetts campuses were second to none in springtime student strikes, campus buildings occupied, and nonnegotiable demands issued. We turned out the biggest crowd in the country on Vietnam War moratorium day, the only rally that day Sen. George McGovern chose to address. Two years later, we were the only state McGovern carried in the most lopsided loss in U.S. history. Well before Nixon's subsequent term was cut short in disgrace, Volkswagens, Volvos, and Saabs across Massachusetts were sporting bumper stickers with smug slogans like "Don't Blame Me, I'm from Massachusetts" and "The One and Only."

Massachusetts boomers grew up feeling special and politically superior, a perception ratified by simple comparisons. Rankings of the nation's smartest populations always put Massachusetts close to the top. While large swaths of America were drawn to the conservative messages of Richard Nixon, George Wallace, and Ronald Reagan ("Ray-gun" to local liberals), prominent Massachusetts politicians of that era included antiwar stalwarts like John Kerry of Vietnam Veterans against the War; liberal technocrat Michael Dukakis from Brookline, where folks balk at pledging allegiance to the flag at town meetings; Ted Kennedy; and Boston's mayor Kevin White, the New Frontier–era populist who was more likely to spend city funds hosting rock concerts than siding with noise-averse bluenoses. "We're gonna tell all our friends at Woodstock, this is the best place there is to play music," said Robbie Robertson of the Band at a 1970 Harvard Stadium concert, an apt testament to the preeminence of our home address.

I know how this inflated the self-esteem of young Massachusetts boomers because I am one of them. I went to private schools with the sons and daughters of the greater Boston intellectual and professional classes, and began my career as a local political journalist after graduating from college in 1977. I've had a box seat for the heyday of the Massachusetts economic "miracle" and the Boston anticrime "miracle," and for their decidedly unmiraculous collapses. I've been up close and personal to John Kerry's quintessentially boomer career, for the full flowering of political correctness in one of its national citadels, for the construction and failure of both an expansive welfare state and history's largest public-works project. I've spent countless hours reporting on the Kennedy legacy, warts and all, from Ted to his congressman nephew, Joe, through a horde of other offspring, hangers-on, and wannabes.

More than forty years after the Camelot analogy was cre-

ated and spun into American political history by a newly widowed but quick-thinking Jackie Kennedy, Massachusetts's love
affair with itself—still robust despite near-daily indictments of
its shallowness—is one of the few remaining artifacts of that
high-flying time. But the sixties are gone, and so is most of the
supporting evidence for Massachusetts exceptionalism. The
state has become an abandoned movie lot where great moments in American civic life and modern-day political liberalism were once played out, but no more.

Despite the unique advantages enjoyed by our moneyed
classes, such as the superior health care provided by our world-
class teaching hospitals, those benefits don't trickle down to the
common man and woman the way some liberals imagine.
Even as local bureaucrats struggled to find a way to provide
the low-cost coverage promised in the state's heavily hyped
universal health insurance plan, a late 2006 study found costs
for the average worker's health care had soared to nearly
$10,000 a year, fourth-highest in the nation. "Labor is strong,
so benefits tend to be rich," noted one health-care analyst.
"High-end providers such as teaching hospitals have higher
unit costs for surgery, and there are many insurance benefits
mandated by the state." Yet unless you already have one, good
luck finding the stable white-collar jobs needed to keep up
with such spiraling costs. Traditional manufacturing long ago
fled south and west, followed by alarming numbers of Massachusetts residents. Our vaunted universities fueled a technology sector boom in the 1980s known as the "Massachusetts
Miracle." But the boom faded by the early 1990s and went
completely bust at the turn of the century; in the last recession

the state lost nearly 150,000 jobs in the tech sector and the professional and business services that feed off it, and only a fraction of those have been recovered. Software and medical labs may still turn out the occasional breakthrough, but chances are the products they yield will be manufactured in other states with lower taxes and higher profit margins.

The high-tech industry that temporarily fueled the boom before it went bust has since found the economic and political climates in North Carolina, Texas, and even blue, high-cost California more to its liking, for good reason. A 2005 report card by the nonpartisan Government Performance Project gave Massachusetts poor grades, scolding state government for providing "no true statewide capital plan [or] forward-looking comprehensive workforce plan . . . sporadic strategic planning and performance measurement . . . minimal statewide planning." The result? After two decades of Democratic rhetorical homage to the need for enhanced economic competitiveness, a 2006 study by a Boston think tank found that "on average Massachusetts firms have costs 20–30% higher than similar companies in Texas, North Carolina and New Hampshire in nine key industries."

Meanwhile, Massachusetts leads the nation in precious few measurements of economic dynamism. We are only the nation's thirteenth largest state, but rank fifth in median housing costs, ninth in per-capita state and local tax burden, ninth-worst in economic burden on small business. We have the fourth-highest average auto-insurance and natural-gas bills, the sixth-highest electricity prices. Caught in the pincer of soaring costs and stagnant incomes, Massachusetts residents grasp at straws; we spend more on lottery tickets than do all but four other states, a desperate $681 per capita extracted almost entirely from folks who can ill afford it. In the contemporary annals of state-level political and economic success stories, we are yesterday's liberal newspaper in a new world where both newspapers and liberalism seem to be on life support.

But Massachusetts does set the national pace in one unfortunate area: the development and export into the Democratic Party mainstream of bogus political strategies and practices that misjudge, offend, and ignore the very voters to whom Democrats stake the most passionate claim. In his vivid analysis of the nation's reddest state, *What's the Matter with Kansas?* journalist Tom Frank spoke for boomer liberals everywhere when he puzzled over working-class voters "getting their fundamental interests wrong" by siding with wedge issue–wielding Republicans. "For us it is the Democrats that are the party of workers, of the poor, of the weak and the victimized," he wrote. "Understanding this, we think, is basic; it is part of the ABCs of adulthood." Add a *D* to that alphabet—for delusional.

Democrats and their sympathizers can look through the microscope at Massachusetts and see the failures that have too often critically compromised the contemporary liberal argument. Chief among these is the eyebrow-raising gap, often invisible to boomer Democratic leadership, between their cushy lifestyles and those of the folks they purport to champion, and the corresponding chasm between their promises and performance.

For a state chock-full of liberals who love to rant about

what Ted Kennedy calls America's "shameful" gulf between the haves and have-nots, Massachusetts under liberal boomer stewardship has a lot of explaining to do. According to a recent study by the Massachusetts Budget and Policy Center, a liberal think tank, the earnings gap between wealthy and low-income families grew over the past twenty years at a faster pace here than in all but two other states, New York and Arizona. Billions of dollars in spending on education and child welfare haven't spared Massachusetts from the nation's largest gap between the standard of living of low-income and middle- to high-income children. For those lucky enough to afford one of the state's upper-tier colleges and graduate schools, and for the skilled financial-service or medical specialists holding six-figure jobs in Boston's elite brokerage firms and hospitals, life here is sweet, a question of which hip restaurant to patronize this weekend. But the average family in the bottom fifth of wage earners is pulling down seven times less than the top earners, with little or no upward movement in their wages. Local researchers say the state's median annual earnings, adjusted for inflation, have risen a microscopic 1.2 percent since 1989, even as productivity has been goosed by 50 percent. For fifty-four-year-old Felicity Rivera, a widowed Puerto Rican immigrant raising two teenagers, that means a losing battle to get by on her minimum-wage machine operator's job with a Worcester plastics manufacturer. "It's so hard keeping up with the cost of living," she told a reporter. "Everything goes up every year, except my wages." The benefits of the state's extraordinary intellectual assets "have not been evenly shared in the last 20 years," concluded the Massachusetts Budget and Policy Center study. The inequities of capitalism and the pressures of globalization are everywhere, but Massachusetts "has more extreme versions of trends that were happening nationally."

And the sorry truth is that the anguish of being left off the gravy train extends well beyond Massachusetts's poorest to the likes of Carrie Sylvester, a divorced mother of two with a good white-collar job as an Internet publisher and a home in a bucolic coastal suburb of Boston. "I never expected to live large in this state," she told a local newspaper. But with constant upward pressure on the cost of living, most notably through a property-tax burden exacerbated by soaring home values and the insatiable demands of municipal budgets, it's all she can do to keep up her mortgage payments. "I just want to get by, and it's almost impossible to do it. The cost of everything around here is crazy."

It was his vague but tantalizing promise to relieve property-tax pressure that helped elect Deval Patrick governor in the fall of 2006. Patrick, the former top civil rights official in the Clinton administration's Justice Department, was handsome, poised, and an elegant articulator of Kennedy-era imagery. Citing his rise from the slums of Chicago to Harvard Law School and beyond, Patrick cast his candidacy as a beacon of "hope" for the state's downtrodden. "I don't have the insider connections and the money the other candidates do," he told an enthralled crowd of liberals at the state Democratic convention. "But what I do have is a plan to move us forward, and the life and leadership experience to make it real."

During the campaign against Republican Lt. Gov. Kerry Healey, polls showed the voters preferred Healey's positions to Patrick's on a range of hot-button topics, from denying driver's licenses to illegal immigrants to allowing broad public access to criminal-offender records. But taxes and the overall economic/cost-of-living climate were the big issues. While Healey hammered away at Patrick for opposing a state income-tax rollback that voters had called for in a 2000 referendum, Patrick countered that easing the property-tax burden was more important, even if it meant keeping the extra income-tax revenue and funneling it to cities and towns to help relieve their budgetary stress. By nearly a two-to-one margin, voters agreed.

It's unclear, to say the least, if Patrick has any hope of delivering on his sales pitch. As he took office in January 2007, the state was looking at a billion-dollar budget deficit. But if he can't deliver, while the beleaguered middle- and lower-classes of Massachusetts may be disappointed, few will be surprised. While Ted Kennedy issues press releases from the compound in Hyannisport blaming the working classes' distress on stingy Republicans and Patrick retreats to his 10,000-square-foot summer mansion in the Berkshires—dubbed the "Taj Deval" by a competitor in the Democratic primary—to mull his unfulfilled promises, Cynthia Bashaw of Byfield, a rural town in the state's "drive-by" midsection that the Boston elites whiz by on the way to their vacation homes, will be nursing her hard-earned cynicism. One morning during the governor's race, Bashaw saw an aerial photo of the Taj Deval in the newspaper and was moved to write a letter to the editor. "I was at the grocery store trying to figure out how to make the $76.24 in my checking account feed my family of five for five days until my next paycheck. The story made me wonder what kind of principles and philosophy guide a man who builds such a house in a world of need."

Bashaw's skepticism proved warranted weeks before Patrick took office, when he stunned even his most ardent supporters by unveiling plans for a weeklong series of inaugural events costing well over a million dollars, far more than had ever been spent on a Massachusetts gubernatorial inauguration; donations from corporate lobbyists were "capped" at $50,000. Wrote one local newspaper editorialist: "This is a celebration more fit for a king than governor of the commonwealth."

Egomania and the shameless bait and switch have been consistent characteristics of liberal boomer stewardship of Massachusetts. "Mike Dukakis doesn't just talk about Democratic values," read a 1988 Dukakis-for-president brochure. "He puts them into action." The Dukakis campaign went a long way on the promise of a national version of the Massachusetts Miracle, and it sounded just swell. "Mike Dukakis believes Americans, no matter where they live, want the same things for themselves and their families: good jobs at good wages, good schools for their children, decent housing, safe and attractive neighborhoods, affordable health care, a clean environment. Above all, they want a strong and thriving economy."

But even as Dukakis was getting waxed by George H. W. Bush in the 1988 election, the phoniness of the "miracle" was being exposed for all to see. An unsupportable state budget

pumped full of pork-barrel spending on overpriced consultants and patronage hacks collapsed in a heap of social-service
cutbacks and tax hikes. Bush famously lampooned Dukakis's
mediocre environmental record by campaigning on a boat in
filthy Boston Harbor. A universal health-care plan hustled
through the legislature to give candidate Dukakis a campaign
talking point was later scrapped for lack of funds, a precursor,
perhaps, to the dubious future of the current health-care
scheme.

As he accepted his party's nomination in 1988, Dukakis
told the nation the choice was about "competence," not ideology. But when it comes to providing opportunity and hope for
the masses, the competence of Massachusetts political elites,
then and now, is highly suspect at best. Census research shows
more than 230,000 people fled the state between 2000 and 2005
in search of stable, well-paying jobs and decent, affordable
housing. "They want a yard, they want a home, they want to
have the American dream," said one demographic expert reviewing the exodus data. "And it's persistently unaffordable in
Massachusetts."

If the facts of who doesn't prosper in the bluest state aren't
enough to undercut liberal boomer credibility, the sight of
who is benefiting seals the indictment. In his 1964 book *The
Pursuit of Justice*, Bobby Kennedy wrote: "The problem of
power is how to achieve its responsible use rather than its irresponsible and indulgent use—of how to get men of power to
live for the public rather than off the public." Kennedy's
epiphany has been a crucial part of the liberal self-image as

reformist and populist; forty years later, star consultant Robert Shrum was still channeling the notion of Democrats "fighting" for "the people versus the powerful" through John Kerry, his seventh consecutive losing Democratic presidential candidate.

For a generation that fancies itself reinventing everything, including history, another quote is worth recalling: George Santayana's admonition that "those who cannot remember the past are condemned to repeat it." Kennedy's musings on the proper priorities for the powerful were an echo of the Radical Republicanism of another idealistic generation a century ago: "A hearty faith in the great principles of popular government, a generous hospitality toward new views and constant progress, a practical perception of the close relation between morals and politics, a deep conviction of the vital necessity of intelligence to a true republic."

In Massachusetts, that altruistic impulse has long since dissolved into an orgy of spoils taking. In the impoverished immigrant city of Lawrence, where a tiny percentage of the mostly poor and Latino students have a shot at a college degree, badly needed state education funding was diverted into frills like a customized SUV for the superintendent (with an extra step built in to help his wife hop aboard) and a laptop for the high-school janitor. The state's Democratic establishment (often with the eager collaboration of Republican governors) turned supposedly independent authorities overseeing Logan Airport and the Big Dig into vast patronage buffets, where otherwise unemployable relatives of the politically connected found safe harbor, and former state legislators could pad their pensions in overpaid make-work jobs with perks that rival those of the most rapacious corporations.

These feeding frenzies cost the taxpayers more than money. World Trade Center bombing mastermind Mohamed Atta and his colleagues breezed through Logan checkpoints on September 11, 2001, just a few months after political appointees masquerading as managers failed to act on an airport security official's urgent memo warning of lax passenger screening. Two of the plane-bombs of September 11 took off out of Logan that day. The hack-o-rama at the Massachusetts Turnpike Authority was so indifferent to quality control on the Big Dig that loose bolts holding three-ton panels to the ceiling of one of its tunnels were reinforced with duct tape or left uninspected. After a bolt gave way in 2006, killing a woman in a car below, thousands of defects were found in tunnel construction left largely uninspected by its caretakers.

But the Massachusetts power brokers responsible for these travesties angrily reject any personal accountability. When Ted Kennedy, John Kerry, and other top Democrats met with reporters after the Big Dig tunnel collapse, I had a testy exchange with Rep. Michael Capuano—a vociferous critic of the Bush administration's reluctance to own up to its Iraq war failures—that typifies the local establishment's unwillingness to acknowledge its own culpability.

"Looking for heads on the wall, that's all well and good and that's fine, but it's not gonna help this particular situation," he snapped, when I asked why they hadn't properly overseen the project.

"That's what accountability is, sir," I suggested.

"I disagree."

Time to invoke Santayana. "If we don't understand and admit the mistakes of the past, aren't we condemned to repeat them?"

Capuano squinted sullenly. "I don't know what you mean by that."

The political elites may be in denial about the state's downward spiral, but ordinary citizens are voting with their feet in startling numbers. In a 2006 survey of Massachusetts expatriates, half fingered exorbitant housing costs as their main reason for moving out, 30 percent singled out high taxes, and 26 percent cited liberal politics as a significant negative. Blue-collar respondents were likelier to cite crime and failed political leadership; 92 percent were happy they fled. Asked what they missed most about Massachusetts, about a quarter cited family members. The same number referenced the natural surroundings. The next most popular answer was "nothing."

The following chapters present one boomer's account of what's wrong with Massachusetts, a tale that might prove instructive to Capuano and other naked emperors of the baby boom generation. In this saga of self-indulgence, unchecked egotism, do-as-I-say-not-as-I-do hypocrisy, political correctness, and affectation, they may learn why much of the rest of the country is doubled over as they parade by in what they imagine to be regal political finery. News flash: the onlookers are laughing sarcastically, not bowing with respect. It's the story of well-educated, mostly well-intentioned political leaders, gifted with a rare chance to implement their idealistic visions, who have squandered much of their capital in a narcissistic binge. And most of all, it's an urgent, cautionary tale for a generation that's at dire risk of winding up like Bill McKay, the self-absorbed idealist Robert Redford played in *The Candidate,* a Kennedy caricature who loses his moral and ethical bearings in pursuit of power, only to sit on the edge of a hotel bed at his own victory party and ask woefully, "What do we do now?"

CHAPTER TWO

....

Rob and Alison

ROB WAS AN outgoing young guy from Melrose, a small blue-collar city of about 28,000 just a few miles north of Boston. Alison, from East Boston, an immigrant community of close-knit families like hers, was quieter than Rob and six years younger. They met and fell in love when they both worked at the East Boston Neighborhood Health Center, commiserating with each other about the hassles of trying to deliver health care to a huge, needy population.

Rob left the health center in 1999 to go into more lucrative work with an assisted-living development firm. But his heart had been set on a career in government through a hard-earned bachelor's in political science from Fordham and a master's in public administration from Northeastern. Both his grandfather, a school custodian, and his father, a teacher, had done well on the public payroll. The grandfather had a summer house in

New Hampshire; his mother didn't work, yet there was money for nice vacations each year. Alison understood his career decision. Her father was a mailman, and she appreciated both public service and the benefits its employees enjoy.

Rob's $80,000 a year isn't chump change. Combined with the $30,000 Alison makes from her health-care work, the couple are well ahead of the $78,000 median income in Melrose, where in 2002, after months of looking, they finally found a house they could afford. Fourteen Haywood Street is a modest but immaculate colonial on a dead-end street. The previous owners put in a nice new kitchen, and the yard is big enough for a kid and a dog to get dirty in. When Alison and Rob pulled up the carpeting, the hardwood was in great condition. Now the bad news: the floor is in far better shape than Rob and Alison's finances—and nerves. Sitting at their dining-room table, with eighteen-month-old Ryan winding Thomas the Tank Engine around their feet, Rob grimly recites the details of his financial obligations.

"We paid $380,000 for it, stole it for $380,000," he says. "If we didn't come in at just the right time, they could have got $420,000, easy. We barely pulled it off. Who has twenty percent to put down on a house? We were able to put down seven percent with help from both sets of parents, plus we had our wedding money saved." He shakes his head and looks out the window, as if reality might be coming up the walk to rescind his lucky break. "I can't imagine what people who didn't have that perfect storm can do."

Suffer in a lesser place or throw money away on rent, if they're lucky. The next county over, Essex County, with only a slightly higher median home price than Melrose, topped the 2006 Forbes.com list of the ten most overpriced places in the United States. If the sky-high cost of living and low salaries don't throttle you financially, sparse job growth and scarce affordable housing will, Forbes found. "While there is no dearth of wealth in those areas, ordinary folk may be squeezed" was Forbes's polite comment.

The squeeze on Rob and Alison isn't a matter of delaying a Caribbean vacation or eating at fancy restaurants less often. Those frills were never in the picture. "Good child care costs seventy dollars a day," he says, a problem for them, an insurmountable hurdle to many others. The most recent research by the nonprofit advocacy group Massachusetts Citizens for Children estimated more than 500,000 kids in the state needed some form of day care, but for their working-class parents "the cost can easily exceed rent and car payments."

Rob brings home $4,000 a month after taxes; Alison kicks in $890 every other week. They're brown-bagging it at work, keeping debt low, and living frugally at home. Laments Rob, "My job prevents me from taking a second job." Meanwhile, a gallon of heating oil, which ran about $1.42 a couple of years ago, is up to $2.41 by late 2006 even after a couple of unusually mild winters. They're still paying off Alison's 2004 Subaru, but thank God, Rob has managed to pay off the loan on his 2000 Dodge Neon, a car so hideous his buddies joke that its purpose is to make people think he's humble. Even with the loan paid off, there's the insurance: $2,400 a year on the two cars. Massachusetts drivers pay the nation's fourth-highest insurance rates, 27 percent more than the average driver elsewhere, in part because we file nearly twice as many property-damage claims as the average American and nearly three times as many bodily injury claims.

Everywhere Rob and Alison look, they see couples like themselves, solidly middle-class by any measure, getting by only because they have extended family to lean on. "There's an army of grandparents taking care of their grandkids, a generation of them." Rob glances at Alison before confiding that the financial pressure may wind up "limiting having another child. Without the parents to help, I don't know what we'd do. We'd be poor."

For this Generation X couple, "the line between being okay and being lost is this thin," says Rob, holding his thumb and forefinger just barely apart. Recently, they took a frightening swerve onto the rumble strip. Alison complained of a low-grade fever. A 13-centimeter tumor was found on her lymph nodes. After three weeks of looking into the abyss—"the worst experience of my life," says Rob—the biopsy came back negative, but surgery had to be performed, and Alison was out of work for three months. Their savings account dipped below $1000. "I couldn't help thinking, what if something goes wrong with the roof? What if something happens to the boiler?" Rob recalls.

Little Ryan has dozed off on the living-room floor, and the conversation about Rob and Alison's fragile budget has trailed off into anxious silence. But the couple's animation returns when I ask what Kennedy country should be doing to help ease the burden for working families. They're both from staunchly Democratic families. Their grandparents have pictures of JFK up in the parlor, right alongside the pope. To their boomer parents, "Republicans are bad, and Ronald Reagan was the devil." Yet they have nothing good to say about the welfare state their Democratic boomer elders have created. "Growing up in East Boston, you have to struggle, and you see people abuse the system because they can, [because] it's allowed," says Alison, as she and Rob recall the "thousands and thousands" of people they believe abused the free services at the East Boston healthcare center. "We should work harder to not enable people." They wonder why some of the "disabled" clients they saw, able-bodied but purportedly suffering from bipolar disorder and collecting thousands in benefits, can't help ease the tax burden by taking on at least part-time work. "They should encourage the people to work instead of just giving them money," suggests Alison.

She's echoing a complaint that's been pouring out of working-class Massachusetts for decades. In 1987, as an editor for a chain of weekly newspapers, I got a tip from a state welfare department employee furious about local welfare-approval mills. I sent a robustly healthy twentysomething reporter to the offices of two local doctors he had identified, armed with welfare forms and a vaguely scripted story about "not feeling well." Both times, he walked out after cursory "examinations" (one of the doctors didn't even have him take off his shirt), having exchanged cash for a signed form certifying him medically unable to work and qualified for over $10,000 in benefits. Three years later, then Boston University president John Silber became a major contender in the gubernatorial race after noting a huge influx of immigrants into some blue-collar cities and questioning generous state welfare policies that he claimed had turned the state into "a welfare magnet." Appalled, local liberals nearly knocked him off the ballot at the state convention. But Silber pulled Reagan Democrats into the primary and won the nomination in a walk, losing narrowly in the final election.

Voter clamor for welfare reform reached a peak in 1994 when the *Boston Globe* reported on the family background of Clarabel Ventura, a drug addict who had been arrested for severely injuring her four-year-old son. Ventura was one of fourteen children born to a Puerto Rican immigrant living off welfare, the tip of a dependency iceberg that extended through seventy-four grandchildren and fifteen great-grandchildren. Total cost to beleaguered taxpayers: up to a million dollars a year. The story was cited on the floor of the U.S. Senate as a classic case study of never-ending welfare abuse, and played a role in the passage of sweeping federal welfare reform in 1996. Back in Massachusetts, liberals were dismissive of the outcry. "Should we have forced sterilization like the white racists in the deep South proposed a hundred years ago?" said one. "The system does perpetuate a cycle of dependency, and this family is clearly a dramatic example of that," conceded David Cortiella, director of the Boston Housing Authority. "I will get in a lot of trouble with my liberal friends for saying that, but it is true."

In the end, modest welfare reforms were passed in Massachusetts, driven in part by the memorable statement of Clarabel's sister Maribel, herself the beneficiary of thousands in welfare benefits because of "anxiety attacks" that leave her unable to work. Asked to comment on the anxiety of working people fed up with paying her family's freight, Maribel's message was succinct: "Just tell them to keep paying." A decade later, the welfare rolls are down, but reform still rankles Beacon Hill liberals. In 2006 the legislature's refusal to toughen work requirements for welfare recipients cost the state close to $60 million in federal aid.

But while Rob shares Alison's disdain for welfare abuse, it's the entitlement-fueled greed of middle-class boomers that especially galls him. "People in this state have become almost dependent on the state to take care of their problems. We have so many different programs here," he says. "You have a group a little older than us who want to pay just so much in taxes, they want high-class public schools and every park a gem, but they don't want to pay for what they get. The elderly, the World War II generation, they built themselves from nothing, and now even for them, everything's based on entitlement. We have all sorts of antidrug programs. Even in schools there's a program for every child." And for some children with broadly defined "special needs," outlandishly expensive "special education" programs are demanded by their boomer parents. During the late 1990s, special-education spending grew far faster than the overall per-student public expenditure rate, and the public costs of pacifying some litigious parents hit six figures.

Rob doesn't quite get it about the boom generation running the show here. "They came of age with [John F.] Kennedy and were questioning toward government during Vietnam and after Watergate, fine. But then they became reliant on government, and they created a program for everything, all these unfunded mandates on local government to take care of everyone under the sun who had some sort of issue. This group hated government, they got elected to completely reform the government, but they ended up being worse than the people they threw out."

Rob's work sometimes requires him to travel to Beacon Hill for meetings or hearings, and he abhors every trip. "They totally don't get it about what's going on on Main Street, and the Democrats are just as bad as the Republicans." A self-proclaimed reformist generation has turned the public payroll into a costly fiefdom as self-serving as anything James Michael Curley or Tammany Hall's Boss Tweed might have imagined, he believes. With powerful public-employee unions making sure the legislature doesn't rock the boat, "they've set up a lucrative pension system, they pay almost nothing for health care," says Rob. The lavish benefits package—most public employees pay only 15 percent of their health-care premium—critically squeezes municipal budgets, choking the schools, and social services it pays for. But when Melrose officials ask the unions for more equitable cost sharing, "they get nuts. They don't even want to talk about paying more," reports Rob. When he looks at a calcified political establishment—where there hasn't been an incumbent Democratic congressman unseated since 1992 and officeholders in general age unimpressively in place like the picture of Dorian Gray—Rob sees a generation circling the wagons around its ill-gotten gain. "New people with fresh ideas should be called on to be the next generation of leadership, but they're so afraid someone might upset the apple cart."

That fear is a potent political tool in Massachusetts. During the 2006 gubernatorial race, GOP nominee Kerry Healey proposed to reform the state's Rube Goldberg setup of 106 separate tax-funded pension systems, inept generators of $13 billion in unfunded liability. Radical concepts like "consolidation" and "eliminating abuses" were floated, and Healey even called for public employees to pay 25 percent of their healthcare premiums. The need for pension reform is recognized nationally as one of the most serious threats confronting boomer retirees. Thomas J. Healey of Harvard's Kennedy School of Government, an assistant secretary of the Treasury under Ronald Reagan, argues that the boomers are headed for a $1 trillion nightmare of unfunded pension liability that will make the $200 billion savings-and-loan bailout of the 1980s seem like child's play in terms of destroyed retirements and shattered lives. But parts of his answer—"benefit reductions" and defined-contribution plans that would cut the "generous pension allowances that state plans are ill-equipped to afford"— are a complete nonstarter under the Massachusetts model. The unions trashed Kerry Healey's modest plan in harsh terms. "This is nothing more than trying to play on anti–public employee sentiment like the Republican party has been doing for the last several decades," Rich Marlin, the top lobbyist for the Massachusetts AFL-CIO, told me. "No one's gonna be able to afford to work for the state, which is maybe what their ultimate goal is, to keep anyone from working here."

Democratic nominee Deval Patrick laid low on the subject. And the brass at unions like the 3,000-member Massachusetts Association of State Engineers and Scientists (MOSES) made sure their members knew what to do on Election Day to continue on their journey to the promised land. "It seems that the trend to balance the state budget on the backs of its employees will continue if Kerry Healey is elected," wrote a columnist in the *MOSES Monitor* newsletter. "If you don't wish to fund these initiatives with your paycheck, please help by educating your family and friends about the real truth and encourage them to vote for Deval Patrick."

In Rob's experience, when local Democratic political elites aren't playing defense against badly needed modernization, they're choking off the party's future by promoting "fierce, angry partisanship" that turns off him and his peers. Twice in the past three years he's been stripped of his status as a delegate to the state Democratic convention because he supported the popular incumbent state senator for Melrose, a bright young progressive Republican named Richard Tisei. Rob says Tisei has been ultraresponsive anytime the city needs something handled on Beacon Hill. "I'm going to support the person who best represents my community," says Rob. "Sometimes that isn't a Democrat. That doesn't make me disloyal or a traitor." His party's insistence that it does is emblematic, he says, of a political attitude that "is destroying the country in terms of policy, and it's one of the reasons that people my age aren't getting involved in politics."

Rob fondly recalls the middle-class upbringing his parents gave him here, but sees the future he once dreamed of for his own son slipping away. Melrose is bordered by the 2,575-acre Middlesex Fells, the largest public park north of Boston, once a beautifully maintained maze of cleared trails where Rob and his friends spent unsupervised 1980s afternoons playing hide-and-seek. Now, he laments, many of the trails are obscured by tangled underbrush, and parts of the park are dangerous for kids. From his desk at city hall, he sees an ever-tightening fiscal squeeze on services that mirrors his own family's predicament in both its relentlessness and the boom generation's failure to do anything about it. "We've closed two elementary schools in five years" due to inconsistent state aid, lack of new growth, and soaring fixed costs, he reports. "Do you know what that does to our psyche? There's very little business here, the neighborhood schools are the hubs of the community. It is like ripping the soul out of a neighborhood."

If he had to be party to another school closing, vows Rob, he'd rather leave the work he loves. And with a supportive nod from Alison, he acknowledges thinking the unthinkable—following the path of so many of his peers out of state in search of a better life in a less economically moribund, politically hidebound backwater.

"People were always willing to pay more to live here," he says. "We had the best education, the best culture and recreational opportunities. We were the closest thing to Europe in America. We invested in our architecture and ourselves. We were the innovators in medicine, business, technology, research. All the great things were invented here, public education, modern policing, libraries. You would go to other parts of the country and you just wouldn't see all that in one place; that was the big difference between us and everywhere else. But the big thing is, we've gone down and everyone else has caught up."

We talk about the rosy economic spin from Beacon Hill boomers. Just as the high-tech bubble helped make up for the collapse of manufacturing in the 1980s they say, and the Internet bubble perked things up in the mid-1990s, something else will soon come along—a new wave of biotechnology products, or miracle drugs created by stem cell research—that will make Massachusetts a mecca again for investment and job growth. Rob just laughs. Why manufacture anything here in high-tax, unaffordable Massachusetts when you can harvest the fruits of your research here and turn them into profits in a state or country with a fraction of the overhead? When it comes to lifestyle, he observes, "The difference between here and Spokane, Washington, or Charleston, South Carolina, or places in Florida is just not that great anymore."

And while the Massachusetts name still evokes travel-brochure visions of bucolic New England landscapes, picket-fence colonial-era neighborhoods clustered around picture-postcard town greens, or throwback industrial cities where abandoned mills have been converted into trendy museums or artists' lofts, that's little more than the photogenic veneer of a Hollywood backlot. Nearly a decade ago the *Globe* documented the grim reality of the "hidden Massachusetts, the tragic, ugly underside" just off the beaten tourist path. In central and western Massachusetts in particular, parts of the state with the misfortune to lie outside the frame of reference of most boom-era power brokers, violent crime and grinding economic and social poverty are staples of daily life. Tobacco Road, meet the picturesque cross-state highway Route 2, "where tourists crowd maple sugar stands, [while in nearby cities and towns] assaults are more widespread than in Boston or Springfield," the *Globe* reported. "South of the Quabbin Reservoir, a stone's throw from antique shops and Old Sturbridge Village, there are towns with more high school dropouts, pregnant teenagers, and families on food stamps per capita than in Brockton or Lynn," two aging eastern Massachusetts cities. Despite state budget growth far in excess of inflation, there are few signs of progress. Statewide, there are more juvenile offenders being ordered to pretrial detention now than there were back then, and central and western Massachusetts still bear the worst of it.

Rob and Alison see Massachusetts boomers clinging delusionally to memories of bygone glory and an enduring myth of superiority. "Like the Celtics of the 1990s, growing old with [Larry] Bird, [Kevin] McHale, and [Robert] Parish up front when they can't win anymore," offers Rob. "The boomers are still living in the past. There's an entire generation—my generation—that has never seen the Celtics win a championship. And they have no confidence that we ever will again."

The couple longingly recall the essential American optimism that was conveyed to them by their parents and grandparents, that every generation would do a little better than the last. They bought into it once, and things haven't gone so badly. After all, chunky little Rob Dolan, son of a public-school teacher and grandson of a custodian, had risen at a tender young age to be mayor of Melrose.

But even Rob's realization of that lifelong dream is recalled with palpable bitterness, accompanied by Alison's rueful headshaking. The voters of Melrose like their young mayor just fine, giving him 80 percent of the vote in his most recent reelection, but the political insiders are a different story. "If you're chosen, you're chosen; if you're not, you're locked out," says Rob. "That's how the party works. The people who claim to be the most inclusive are the least inclusive. If I were to say, 'I don't think abortion is right,' that's it, you are an ax murderer as far as most party types are concerned. They would look at you better if you had a syringe in your arm because then you would have a disease they have sympathy for."

Rob is pro-choice, but that hasn't spared him conflicts with the state Democratic hierarchy going back to 1993, when he dared to support the Republican nominee for the open Melrose state representative's seat against an undistinguished Democratic-machine politician. The two previous Democrats to hold the seat had both been forced to resign early due to ethical issues, and the GOP hopeful, an openly gay twenty-five-year-old Italian immigrant's son named Patrick Guerriero, was running as a reformer. During five years at the statehouse and three more as mayor of Melrose, Guerriero's honesty and diligence won him a leadership award from the Kennedy Library and the U.S. Mayor's Association City Livability Award for a "civility initiative" promoting good citizenship. He went on to become national head of the Log Cabin Club, a group of Republicans backing gay rights, and has since switched his registration to Democrat in disgust over the GOP's antigay stance. But the boomer activists who dominated the local Democratic apparatus never forgave Rob for backing Guerriero. "I was yelled at, labeled 'not a loyal Democrat,' someone who 'could not be trusted,'" he recalls. "That label got up to the highest levels of the party." When he ran for mayor the first time in 2001, the Democratic State Committee didn't give him a penny. He financed his shoestring campaign with $25-a-head fund-raisers where "everyone was either my age, or 80."

Rob and Alison Dolan see too many Massachusetts boomers indulging their egos, shirking their duty to family and community, bungling their leadership duties, and draining public resources by operating under the premise that, as Rob puts it, "the more you scream and yell, at a teacher or at government, the more you'll get." They look at boomer elders in power and see disinterest in the serious prioritization and reform that they think state government needs. Beyond their own plight, they sense a general "disdain for working people." Alison says her disappointment in local boomer leadership has led her to vote Republican at times, and she sees little hope for improvement. "When I look at that generation now, it's scary."

And as the mayor of Melrose helps his wife put their son to bed, he admits to being frightened of the future as well, a middle-class lament heard from coast to coast that has gone unanswered in the bluest state. "My biggest fear is I won't be able to provide Ryan with the opportunity that I had," says Rob. "In terms of being keepers of the flame, this group hasn't been able to keep it. So it's our responsibility to reclaim it. But the problem is, how many people who have the ability to reclaim it have left Massachusetts already?"

CHAPTER THREE

....

"A Pizza a Week"

THE FORCES OF truth and justice were on the march in
Marblehead, an old harbor town north of Boston that played a
key role in the American Revolution. Marblehead sailors, organized into a crude fighting force by General John Glover,
formed the first ranks of the American navy here. The men of
the Fourteenth Continental Regiment would later become famous for their role in George Washington's crossing of the
Delaware River, a turning point in the Revolutionary War that
freed the New World from taxation without representation.

But on a fall day more than two centuries later, Marblehead was host to a strikingly different sort of rebellion. The
two dozen marchers parading through the historic streets
were almost all women, welfare mothers bused in from
gritty urban neighborhoods by the Tri-City Welfare Rights
Organization (WRO). Some had small children in tow. One

pregnant teen pushed her one-year-old in a stroller. Most lived in state-subsidized welfare motels. All shared one common denominator—anger over an ongoing petition drive to roll back a series of recent statewide tax hikes.

The tax increases were the work of lame-duck governor Michael Dukakis and the Democratic legislature, necessary in part, so they claimed, to cover the soaring costs of the generous Massachusetts welfare system. Since the 1960s, benefits had mushroomed to 40 percent more than the national median. One study found 71 percent of poor children were on welfare, compared with barely 50 percent nationally. That generosity carried a high price tag that was accepted without serious complaint by Massachusetts taxpayers, as long as the economy grew fast enough to feed the beast without boosting tax rates. But the booming state economy of the 1980s, fueled by the computer revolution and high-tech research, had gone bust. Major local employers like Wang Laboratories guessed wrong about the computer industry's future, and were left behind by out-of-state competitors. The Massachusetts academic-research complex was still turning out innovative products, but companies found it far more profitable to manufacture them in other, lower-tax states.

The state's beleaguered working classes, dismayed by a suddenly gloomy economic outlook, weren't reacting well to the tax hikes. Dukakis's approval ratings, depressed by his inept loss in the 1988 presidential race, flatlined locally. Folks weren't amused by the sight of a governor—just back from a national campaign based on the state's alleged economic miracle—making them pay for the miracle's collapse. And as the tax-cut petition gained steam, the marchers of the WRO were feeling under siege by what they termed an attempt to "balance the budget on the backs of the poor, the homeless and the neediest." As they walked, the women and some of their older children clutched a homemade sign: We Look for Justice, but There Is None. We Look for Salvation, but It Is Far from Us.

Finally, the marchers reached their target, the Village Street address of Barbara Anderson. As executive director of Citizens for Limited Taxation (CLT), sponsors of the tax-cut petition, the fast-talking, redheaded Anderson had become the face of the state's surprisingly virile antitax movement. Her group stunned the Democratic establishment by converting outrage over chronic property-tax increases into a 1980 referendum victory that limited tax growth and shifted power over local tax rates from elected officials to voters. They successfully defended the new law against repeated attempts by the state legislature to weaken it, and they played a key role in defeating several efforts to install a graduated income tax. Without the benefit of paid signature gatherers or the large advertising budgets deployed against them by the public-employee unions who fought their every move, Barbara Anderson and CLT had established themselves as the state's most effective check on runaway taxation, far more formidable than the toothless handful of Republicans in the legislature.

So the women of the WRO had come to Marblehead, home to wealthy waterfront property owners and sprawling mansions, intent on demonizing Anderson as a symbol of the obliviousness of the rich to the struggles of the poor. "[They] said they wanted to take their appeal directly to Barbara Anderson's home because they feel that she and others who live in affluent communities like Marblehead live in isolated cocoons divorced from the reality of the majority of the poor and working-class residents of the state," one local newspaper reported. And the letter they carried cast Anderson as no less than a female Ebenezer Scrooge: "You tell people the government doesn't need more money. How can we raise our families if the government doesn't raise taxes? If Massachusetts won't restore services to people like us who depend on them, we would like you to explain how you think we can survive."

But when the marchers arrived on Anderson's street with reporters in tow, their political drama experienced an unexpected plot twist. Anderson, a divorced mother getting by on her modest CLT salary, wasn't in, of course—it was the middle of a workday. And her home was a tiny five-room cottage in need of paint and repair, stuck on a small lot with a view of the street and some tangled underbrush. "Gee," blurted one welfare mom as she surveyed the dump, "I thought the house would be bigger."

Ronald Reagan, Pat Buchanan, or any of the right wing's most accomplished welfare bashers could have had a field day with some of the WRO marchers. The women with the multiple out-of-wedlock offspring pleading poverty when they clearly had never missed a high-calorie meal. The lone man in the group, apparently able-bodied, who told a reporter he couldn't get a job "because I'm too busy running around getting welfare forms and attending rallies for the homeless." These were stereotypical gimme girls and gimme guys, made to order for political manipulators. But in Massachusetts, the political elites don't swap anecdotes about welfare queens, and the taxpayers who vote them in are traditionally generous. The state has a long history of expansive commitment to social welfare. While Reagan and company spent the 1980s trying to rein in entitlements, Dukakis and the all-Democratic power structure were increasing state spending on social services to the poor by 73 percent, and being rewarded for it by the voters with easy reelection.

As the women of the WRO were so shocked to learn when they arrived on the porch of their bête noire, the political resistance confronting the welfare state and its tax-revenue addiction wasn't from rich Uncle Pennybags and other stereotypical mansion dwellers. It was coming from working-class people engaged in an economic struggle of their own, folks like Anderson, the daughter of a lumberyard worker from rural Pennsylvania who saved up enough to buy a mom-and-pop hardware store. "I just identify with hard-working people who make it in America and have to struggle," says Anderson, a Navy wife who came to Massachusetts with her husband in 1971. "It wasn't very long before I realized something was very wrong. I had never seen a place where the taxes were so high and the services were so poor. My parents' taxes were relatively low and their services were better. I remember thinking, 'What is wrong with this place?' "

Anderson got her answer out on the campaign trail. Massachusetts voters during the past quarter-century have repeatedly reined in the expansionist plans of liberal Democrats by endorsing CLT-backed tax-cut petitions, but a political establishment that loves to extol the power of the grassroots has never given

the antitax movement even grudging respect. The passage of
the property tax–limiting Proposition 2½ in 1980 has been cited
by nonpartisan observers for unlocking the state's economic potential by stabilizing tax rates and forcing much-needed accountability on profligate local officials. It is even credited with
improving public education in one state study by giving schools
a strong incentive to "deliver quality education in order to raise
property values" and thus generate more revenue without raising the tax rate. While the voters rejected the 1990 CLT petition that brought the protesters out to Anderson's nonpalatial
digs in Marblehead, they passed a state tax-intake cap in 1986
and an income-tax cut in 2000, nearly repealed the income tax
altogether in 2002, and elected three straight antitax Republican
governors. In 2006, amid the healthiest local economy of the decade, two-thirds of the proposed Proposition 2½ overrides were
defeated by local voters. Said the chairman of the board of se-
lectmen in Newbury, a small suburb north of Boston where
two overrides were rejected in one year, "I've been approached
on the street by citizens saying, 'Stop asking us to raise our
taxes, we are at the end of our rope. How many times do we
have to tell you no?'"

But to a Massachusetts political culture that sees willingness to quietly accept tax hikes as synonymous with good
breeding and spiritual wellness, the Barbara Andersons of the
state are incomprehensible, unacceptable, and vulgar. Anderson recalls one speaking engagement during the 1990 tax battle
in a wealthy suburb stocked with liberal Democrats, where a
bejeweled local matron greeted her with a warning to "be sure
to behave appropriately; this is a high-class group." (Ander-

e ort.

son's tart response: "I don't need any fucking advice on how to give a fucking speech.") Local attempts to override Proposition 2½ often polarize voters along stark class lines: affluent liberals, town officials, public-employee unions, and welfare recipients in favor of the tax hike; senior citizens, entrepreneurs, middle- and lower-income working people opposed. It's a perpetual rerun of the political realignment pulled off by the Reagan revolution, the cleaving of the old New Deal Democratic coalition by casting government as an effete bureaucratic corps hell-bent on imposing an insatiable drain on the economic well-being of the working classes. The way Anderson and her allies see it, theirs is a battle between the beleaguered worker and an unholy alliance of "the people who take advantage of the services and wealthy people without any understanding of the working class."

Massachusetts liberal elites do their best to confirm the antitax movement's darkest suspicions about them. Anderson once saw a pro-tax liberal lecture an elderly woman who complained she couldn't cover her living costs on a fixed income: "If you can't afford to pay your property taxes, then you're probably not managing your portfolio correctly." During an override battle in Natick, a tony Boston suburb, a tax-hike supporter wrote a letter to the local paper contending that opponents could easily find the money to pay a higher tax rate if they'd only give up their "cigarettes and Lottery tickets." Over the years, taxpayers have been treated to a string of condescending euphemisms from opponents of proposed tax cuts. To this day, tax hikes are referred to in polite circles as "revenue enhancements," as if the boobs in the street will open their wallets if they think they're paying for state-budget breast augmentation. But tax cuts are never acknowledged as potential "enhancements" to the workingman's quality of life. One proposed cut was said by opponents to be worth merely "a Coke a week" to the average family. Another was dismissed as "a pizza a week." Both passed easily. Liberals incredulous at the apparent greed of this junk food–swilling electorate "have never sat at the kitchen table on a Friday night counting the nickels and dimes in the cookie jar to see if you can afford that pizza, or maybe pepperoni to go on it," suggests Anderson. "People like Ted Kennedy can relate to the poor, but they can't relate to people like us."

The recurring character trait that perhaps alienates voters most of all is the do-as-I-say, not-as-I-do mentality of the ruling elites. Massachusetts boomer liberals never tire of scolding tax-resistant citizens for their "compassion fatigue." The state's largest teachers' union regularly runs TV ads featuring wide-eyed schoolkids begging for more "investment" in their future. Swallow your economic anxiety and give up more of your income "for the children," taxpayers are told.

Whatever guilt this may inspire in taxpayers is quickly dispelled by the behavior of supposedly pro-tax liberals, who do their share to help earn Massachusetts its ranking as one of the nation's least charitable states. Even accounting for a post–September 11 uptick in donations here, the annual *Catalogue for Philanthropy* still ranks the state—the third-wealthiest in the nation—close to the bottom in charitable giving, with an average contribution nearly $550 below the national average. And boomer liberals who bemoan the "mean-spiritedness" of their antitax neighbors simply don't put their money where their mouths are. (Or their labor: Massachusetts placed thirty-sixth in the most recent Corporation for National and Community Service rankings of state volunteering rates.)

A few years back, the Democratic legislature was feeling the heat for refusing to comply with the 2000 initiative-petition vote ordering a cut in the state income tax from 5.85 to 5 percent. Amid a budget shortfall, it settled on 5.3 percent instead. But even this modest cut was too much for local liberals, who complained the legislators were not aggressive enough about prompting citizens to "pay their fair share." The backlash irked House and Senate leaders, who allowed a CLT-sponsored amendment to the tax law to pass. The measure allowed any taxpayer concerned about the lower rate to pay the old 5.85 percent levy. In the first year this "generosity for the children" option was available, 843 of the state's two million tax filers opted to pay the higher rate. By 2006, that microscopic number had slipped to 527—one-fortieth of 1 percent of all taxpayers. "What is it with these liberals?" wrote *Boston Herald* columnist Howie Carr. "They're all for everyone paying their fair share, except when it's their turn to buy a round. They're very worried about illegal aliens who don't pay taxes, period, but they care not a whit about lifelong residents in their hometowns who are being driven out by higher property taxes. And now as the check arrives . . . all but 527 liberals in Massachusetts have bolted for the door. Put out an Amber Alert. What about the children?"

In his famous 1980 Democratic Convention speech updating the Kennedy manifesto, Ted Kennedy acted out the

Massachusetts attitude on taxes. In a sneering tone that still infuses the rhetoric of Democrats nationally, Kennedy trashed Ronald Reagan's proposed tax cuts as welfare for the rich, "a wonderfully Republican idea that would redistribute income in the wrong direction. . . . For the few of you, it offers a pot of gold. . . . But the Republican tax cut is bad news for the middle-income families. For the many of you, they plan a pittance of $200 a year, and that is not what the Democratic Party means when we say tax reform." (In 2006 dollars, Kennedy was ridiculing a "pittance" of close to $500.) Four years later, Democratic Party nominee Walter Mondale paid homage to another staple Taxachusetts mantra, that the argument over taxation levels was a stark choice between truth and falsehood. "Whoever is inaugurated in January, the American people will have to pay Mr. Reagan's bills," Mondale said in his nomination acceptance speech. "The budget will be squeezed. Taxes will go up. And anyone who says they won't is not telling the truth to the American people. . . . Let's tell the truth. It must be done, it must be done. Mr. Reagan will raise taxes, and so will I. He won't tell you. I just did."

End result: another crushing Democratic presidential defeat (not to mention the historic, tax cut–fueled economic boom that immediately followed). It has since become conventional wisdom among Democrats that such "candor" is not to be repeated, replaced instead with the embrace of budgeting that "pays as you go" and tax policy that targets that indefinable group known as "working families" for modest cuts, while rejecting "tax breaks for the rich." This fits neatly into the "people vs. the powerful" construct favored by the boom-era's

premier Democratic snake-oil salesman, consultant Robert
Shrum, whose DNA has been found all over a string of fiasco
candidacies from George McGovern's in 1972 to John Kerry's
in 2004. It's no coincidence that Shrum is a protégé of and former aide to Ted Kennedy, nor that the only two Democratic
presidential winners of his time—Bill Clinton and Jimmy
Carter—are the only two candidates he didn't work with.
Shrum's condescending insistence on casting the working
classes as easily exploited boobs content to scramble for the
crumbs rich swine drop as they divide up the tax-cut pie has
long since proven to be, as journalist Michael Barone points
out, "not a winning message." Long ago, "arousing the working masses to claim more money from the evil right was a way
to win elections," but no more. "Clinton understood that the
country and the economy had changed. Bob doesn't get that."

The Shrum-Kennedy neo-populist spin is a tough sell coming from a wealthy Harvard alum like Al Gore, his resur-
rected Tennessee twang notwithstanding, or the richest
member of the Senate, John Forbes Kerry of Massachusetts. In
one memorable 2004 debate moment, Kerry was asked if he
would be "willing to look directly into the camera and, using
simple and unequivocal language, give the American people
your solemn pledge not to sign any legislation that will increase the tax burden on families earning less than $200,000 a
year during your first term?" Replied Kerry, his head franti-
cally swiveling to find the on-air light: "Absolutely. Yes. Right
into the camera. Yes. I am not going to raise taxes." That
painfully contrived vow was easy pickings for George W.
Bush in a subsequent debate. "His rhetoric doesn't match his

record. He has been a senator for 20 years. He voted to increase taxes 98 times. When they tried to reduce taxes, he
voted against that 127 times. He talks about pay-go. I'll tell you
what pay-go means, when you're a senator from Massachusetts, when you're a colleague of Ted Kennedy, pay-go means:
you pay, and he goes ahead and spends." This line of attack is a
cue for appalled eye-rolling among liberal elites, but it works.
As a *Chicago Daily Herald* reader put it in a letter denouncing
Kerry on the eve of the 2004 election: "He will vote no different as president than he did as senator from Taxachusetts."

It's an especially effective stereotype when boomer liberals
inexplicably see no need to repudiate it. The Massachusetts
and federal budgets grow like kudzu, regardless of which
party is in power. But Republicans are more diligent about at
least paying lip service to the idea that waste and fraud con-
sume too many of the working class's hard-earned tax dollars.
Attempts by a string of Republican governors to weed out su-
perfluous state employees or consolidate overlapping agencies
are routinely ridiculed by the Democrats, then left to die in
legislative committee purgatory. And this resistance to fiscal
reform even in times of slack revenues has been the air beneath
Barbara Anderson's wings for more than two decades. "Maybe
you and I can walk and chew gum at the same time, but don't
count on your representatives," she told the crowd at a debate
over one of CLT's tax-cut petitions. "They'll chew the gum
and vote for taxes and forget about everything else—unless we
make them pay attention." In rebuttal that night, Jim Braude, a
lobbyist hired by public-employee unions to counter Anderson's crusade, could only shrug off her complaint: "We have

got to come to the point where we acknowledge no government is waste-free."

Not an especially compelling bumper sticker. And the absence of any real standing with the public as fiscal watchdogs has often left Massachusetts Democrats scrambling for high ground come election time. A notable exception is Deval Patrick, the Democratic governor who made the centerpiece of his 2006 campaign a promise to cut property taxes if voters would reject a further cut in the state income tax. Otherwise there are few instances of carefully crafted "responsible" Democratic rhetoric on taxes convincing a long-skeptical electorate that the whole thing isn't a political charade. And the Patrick breakthrough may prove an isolated exception. Since taking office, Patrick's promise of a property tax cut has been shown to be little more than an expedient campaign sham. Challenged in a private meeting with the state senate president on his claim that $735 million in waste could be squeezed out of the budget, Patrick reportedly told the lawmaker that he "didn't really mean it."

Meanwhile, Anderson says she often receives notes from people fleeing Massachusetts who thank her for her work but say "they can't take it anymore. The high taxes and high cost of living are a problem, but it's the culture they can't take; they just can't stand being pushed around anymore." The people vs. the powerful—if not quite in the way Shrum, Kennedy, and their cronies had in mind.

Massachusetts boomer liberal leadership has developed a culture that ignores the lesson students of the Boston Tea Party learn every day, one coined by a great Massachusetts liberal of his time, the Rev. Jonathan Mayhew: "No taxation without representation." They cannot comprehend the idea that most citizens will pay their fair share without complaint, but not without limit, and most assuredly not without a sense that their money is well spent and their generosity is not exploited. They are oblivious to the notion that resistance to ever-growing tax rates might be something other than the mean-spirited reflex of affluent greedheads. And they cannot countenance the thought that tax resistance might be a backlash of the working classes against elites who take them for chumps, and don't know or care how difficult life is in one of America's costliest states.

"The boom's fixation on self has forged an instinct to make plans or judgments according to wholly internalized standards, based on immutable principles of right and wrong," note Neil Howe and William Strauss, the authors of *Generations: The History of America's Future, 1584 to 2069.* This is certainly true of the Massachusetts attitude toward taxes, where unctuous self-righteousness almost always crowds out political common sense. The phenomenon was on display at a 2006 "interfaith organization rally" held in support of a stiff tax on businesses to fund the proposed Massachusetts universal health-care plan. "Every human being is created in the image of God, and if it's so, then every human body is a sacred vessel," intoned Rabbi Jonah Pesner of Boston's Temple Israel. "Together we will create a coalition of compassion, and we will do what we know to be right, to be just, to be merciful: to bring health-care access and affordability to each and every member of the Commonwealth." Not to be outdone, Rev. Hurmon Hamilton of Roxbury Presbyterian Church announced celestial support for the most draconian tax plan, one proposed by the House Speaker. "God has without doubt been working behind the scenes through the courageous efforts of our speaker," he shouted.

Had such divine endorsement of tax cuts been announced from the pulpit by a conservative preacher, it might have been less glowingly recounted by the *Boston Globe,* which reported Pesner and Hamilton were "waging their fight to expand health care coverage on a different, higher plane." Nonetheless, the story infuriated lawmakers and businesspeople who'd been trying to negotiate a more modest tax structure and didn't appreciate having their spirituality questioned. The ensuing backlash played a role in reducing the business tax in the final bill.

Heading into 2008, there's ample reason to believe that Democrats nationally will either learn from the tax-policy mistakes of Massachusetts liberals, or go down in flames ignoring them. At its annual state trends forum after the 2006 elections, the Council on State Governments cited antitax sentiment as one of its "megatrends" for the near future. In Virginia, antitax sentiment has already killed major tax hikes sought by Democratic governor Tim Kaine, whose 2005 election was seen as an early sign of national Democratic renaissance. Voter resistance will likely harden, suggests Virginia blogger Jim Bacon, who points out that the deflating of the real estate bubble will "portend fiscal problems for local governments which have relied upon soaring property assessments to fund their massive spending increases." For the boomers in charge to belittle that sentiment would be an indulgence in self-defeating, petulant arrogance. But it would also be nothing new. Even a bastion of boomer liberalism such as New York senator Chuck Schumer recalls joining anti–Vietnam War protests as a Harvard undergraduate in the turbulent late 1960s where he was "appalled" by the contemptuous behavior of campus radicals toward blue-collar folks who didn't automatically share their views.

"They'd go over to police officers, right up to their nose, and go 'PIG' so they would hit him, provoke the police officer," remembers Schumer. "And I would go to them and say, 'What are you doing? That guy's trying to earn a living.'"

CHAPTER FOUR

....

Up the Gravity Hill

MARY ANNE MARSH and Barbara Anderson aren't exactly sisters in the struggle. Marsh, a former Massachusetts Democratic activist turned nationally known liberal pundit for the Fox News Channel, has often clashed publicly with Anderson over tax issues. But over miniburgers in a noisy bar near her Back Bay condo, Marsh, an earnest, articulate woman in her late forties, is surprisingly sympathetic to Anderson's view of the Massachusetts political culture. "My concern about the Democrats is when they've had their chance they haven't taken the opportunity to fix the problems people really care about," she says with a mixture of anger and frustration.

Marsh's despair is common among natives of the state's depressed industrial cities. She grew up in Greenfield, a small western Massachusetts community that was once home to the nation's first cutlery factory. The post–World War II rise of low-tax state economies in the South and West and the resulting collapse of Massachusetts's appeal as a manufacturing center decimated Greenfield. Industrial and commercial buildings in the city's once-picturesque downtown were abandoned as the place hemorrhaged jobs. Meanwhile, Greenfield, like much of western Massachusetts, fell off the radar of the state's Boston-centric political elites. While old eastern Massachusetts cities such as Lowell, home to scenic canals and historic old mills, and picturesque Newburyport, a quaint North Shore harbor town, feasted on federal and state redevelopment funds, Greenfield got table scraps. Growing up there, recalls Marsh, "The first thing you learn is Boston is the enemy. They only take from people; you never get anything in return."

Despite that regional skepticism, Marsh was also raised on a classic boomer diet of Kennedy mystique. Her earliest political memory, she recalls, was of John F. Kennedy's assassination and its demoralizing impact on her father, a southern Democrat from a politically active family who moved north to settle down with her Irish Catholic mother. Graduating from Wheaton College south of Boston with a degree in government, Marsh had "a Camelot impression of Democratic politics," a vision of a meritocratic culture where even the idealistic political dreams of a girl from Greenfield could be realized.

Three decades later, we found Marsh picking dispiritedly at her herbed chicken and Asian noodles at a fund-raising luncheon for the Massachusetts Women's Political Caucus, her Camelot dreams in tatters. It was just a few months after another disastrous gubernatorial election for local Democrats. Before the vote, this event had looked like it might be a celebration of a long-overdue breakthrough in the struggle to elect women to high political office here, an uphill battle to say the least. Our top Democrats, liberals all, style themselves as feminists. But you can't help noticing they're all men, masters of a political culture that might as well be a treehouse with a handmade sign on it saying, No Gurlz Allowd. While seventy-eight women across the country held elected statewide executive offices as of the last election, Massachusetts had only one, Republican Lt. Gov. Kerry Healey, who was trounced by Deval Patrick in the 2006 governor's race. The lone woman in statewide office here now is Attorney General Martha Coakley, a Democrat. But three of the five women ever to win a statewide election before her were Republicans, as were two of the three women to hold congressional seats. (The third, Louise Day Hicks, was an archconservative from South Boston who became a national symbol of Boston's at-times violent resistance to court-ordered school desegregation.) The glass ceiling has been only slightly less suffocating in the state legislature. After the 2006 elections, Massachusetts ranked 20th among the states in number of female legislators, lagging badly behind such unprogressive outposts as Kansas, Nevada, and Arizona.

So it was an undeniably historic moment in the fall of 2002 when State Treasurer Shannon O'Brien, an experienced former state rep and senator, finally broke through and beat three men, including the senate president and former U.S. secretary of labor Robert Reich, in the Democratic gubernatorial primary. The morning after the primaries, the pillars of the local Democratic establishment gathered around O'Brien for a celebratory photo op. Among them was House Speaker Tom Finneran, a conservative Democrat by Massachusetts standards from a working-class district in Boston. Finneran saw O'Brien as "a sensible Democrat, not hostile to business, very pleasant, very conversational. No one would describe her as fringe."

Finneran's presence and endorsement were especially important for the party's hopes of ending a twelve-year run of Republican governors. Four years earlier, the speaker, a pro-life, anti–gay marriage Catholic who specialized in preaching to his party about the need for fiscal restraint, had helped torpedo Democratic nominee Scott Harshbarger's run for governor. Harshbarger, the state attorney general, had thrilled the crowd at a postprimary rally in a local union hall by pledging allegiance to the demands of public-employee unions for more state spending. "Labor's agenda is my agenda," he declared. His Republican opponent, incumbent Governor Paul Cellucci, had already been all over him for his adherence to political correctness, most notably the barring of decorative Christmas displays from his employees' cubicles. Finneran had turned out for the Harshbarger rally. But after listening to him endorse the agenda of the same public-employee unions whose relentless budgetary demands Finneran had spent so many hours rejecting, he mused to a reporter that Harshbarger had been captured by "the loony left." The nominee "had allowed a fringe element to dominate the presentation and discussion of issues," Finneran later recalled thinking, a move he bemoaned as political suicide. "The independents are where the swing votes are, and if you're not veering off to the left, the independents will give you the benefit of the doubt." That was

prophetic. On Election Day, the independents broke for Cellucci, and Harshbarger was narrowly defeated.

But four years later, Tom Finneran was there for Shannon
O'Brien. From working with her in the House, he knew her to
be pro-choice, but not extreme about it. Finneran had clashed
with abortion rights activists over their demands for severe restrictions on pro-life demonstrators near abortion clinics, legislation he felt violated the first amendment. "I never remember
Shannon carrying on like that," he says. Culturally, Finneran,
the wisecracking offspring of a South Boston rug cleaner, felt
some affinity for O'Brien, a tough-talking product of East-
hampton in western Massachusetts, the opposite of a boutique
liberal feminist. With her Polish and Irish Catholic roots, she
fit the casting call for a Democratic candidate who could reach
out effectively to the ethnics, moderates, and independents who
had been regularly deserting the party in gubernatorial elections. Party regulars relished the opportunity to finish off Republican nominee Mitt Romney, the Mormon intruder who
had dared to diss Kennedy country in his Senate run eight
years earlier. "She'll stick that quote right up his ass," a top
Democrat assured me on primary night.

O'Brien had paid her dues on Beacon Hill, and the party insiders were behind her. But she had a problem on her left. One
of the also-rans in the Democratic primary, former U.S. labor
secretary Robert Reich, had been the flavor-of-the-summer for
liberals, racking up an impressive 25 percent and needling
O'Brien as insufficiently supportive of abortion rights. While
acknowledging that O'Brien had compiled "a solid pro-choice
voting record" since 1990, one Reich supporter wrote an op-ed

newspaper piece expressing alarm about her 1986 vote in favor of a bill banning abortion except in cases of rape, incest, or danger to the life of the woman. (O'Brien told a reporter back then that "as a Catholic and a public official, I had to balance some differing thoughts.")

For the archliberal *Boston Phoenix,* such past indiscretion, while troubling, was not enough to disqualify her from the holy war against Republicanism. "In some ways, O'Brien is too conservative," the newspaper editorialized. "But she has a marked capacity for growth." And through the first weeks of the general election race, Shannon O'Brien seemed to also have the capacity to win. She dominated early televised debates with Mitt Romney and grabbed an early lead in the polls. She would be in great shape, one of her advisers told me, "once we firm up the liberals."

A month before Election Day, O'Brien was endorsed by Planned Parenthood and the Massachusetts chapter of the National Abortion Rights Action League. Republican pro-choice groups had backed Romney, citing his pledge to preserve the abortion rights status quo in Massachusetts. But that wasn't nearly enough for Melissa Kogut, head of Mass NARAL's political action committee, who called anything short of a vow to push for expansion of abortion rights "dangerous." Accepting the nod from NARAL, O'Brien eagerly seconded that emotion. "I think of the fact that there are people out there who would deprive people of that right to choose," she said. "It is not something that we can take for granted."

It was the start of a world-class squandering of political capital. Romney was zeroing in on the moribund Massachusetts economy, pouring money into TV ads ridiculing O'Brien as a faux moderate passing as a populist while secretly eager to join with a liberal Democratic legislature in an all-out raid on tax-payer earnings. O'Brien continued her awkward pandering to the left, responding to a casual question at an appearance with gay activists with a surprise endorsement of gay marriage. Meanwhile, the hottest item on the ballot after the race for governor was a referendum requiring English immersion for immigrant public-school students, a popular move among urban ethnic Democrats in multilingual neighborhoods. O'Brien, egged on by teacher unions who opposed the ballot question, came out against it.

God is a Mormon! The Romney campaign couldn't believe their good fortune. "O'Brien's lead seems to have evaporated," said one local pollster as voting day approached, observing that the time to move left on hot-button issues was "pre-primary, when she needed those voters. Democrats and Republicans are pretty much spoken for. The key here is wooing the independents." Still, O'Brien held a slim lead in the polls until the night of the final debate, a one-on-one encounter moderated by NBC political analyst Tim Russert. He raised an issue that hadn't come up in previous debates: the age of parental consent for teenage abortions. Massachusetts required it for young women under eighteen, but many abortion rights activists wanted the bar lowered to sixteen. Across the country, even among pro-choice voters, there was widespread support for parental consent rights, anywhere from 65 to 80 percent in most polls. Romney repeated his campaign mantra—no change in existing state law. But O'Brien took the bait. "The age of consent for having sexual relations is lower than the age of 18, so I certainly think that if someone is able to engage in that activity that they should be adult enough to make the decision," she said, parroting the NARAL/Planned Parenthood vision of basic rights under siege. "Understand that this right on the national level is in jeopardy. We need to make sure a woman, every young woman, has the opportunity to control her own health care decisions."

Tim Russert was visibly incredulous. Did O'Brien realize that Massachusetts law required anyone under eighteen to get parental consent for a tattoo? Would she really support a lower standard for abortion? O'Brien, nonplussed, tried to make a joke of it. "Wanna see my tattoo?" she said.

Listening to the debate on his car radio, stopped in traffic in front of St. Ann's Catholic Church in Dorchester, Tom Finneran knew his candidate had stepped in it. "I'm saying to myself, 'Oh my God, oh my God, oh my God, why is she so adamant on this? Why is she worried about pro-choice voters? Where are they gonna go?'" Recalling the episode, Finneran's tone turns woefully sarcastic. "Heaven forbid the parents should know that their little girl is getting an abortion. Shannon knew better, I'm sure of it. But she got put in a corner built by Planned Parenthood, NARAL and the others that doesn't allow anybody a deep breath, doesn't let you meet people in the moderate middle where most people are on abortion."

O'Brien's dismissal of parental consent rights and her flip tattoo comment caused a sensation, and her remarks dominated talk-radio chatter in the campaign's final days. On Election Day, Romney romped. He carried 56 percent of independents, as well as 52 percent of self-described moderates. He mopped up with Catholics, tripling the margin of the previous Republican governor. Despite few endorsements from organized labor, he took 39 percent of union-member votes. But his showing among women was the biggest shocker. Overall, O'Brien carried the women's vote, but her 4-percent margin was the smallest gender gap in years, easily erased by Romney's huge lead among men. And there was an ominous sign for the future: among Generation X women, the Mormon male conservative trounced the Catholic female progressive by 16 points, 57 to 41 percent.

For Mary Anne Marsh, staring despondently at the nonpareil tray at the women's political caucus luncheon, the wound still hadn't begun to scab weeks after the election. To see yet another female candidate fail was "so depressing," she said. "When will it ever end?" Another longtime Democratic Party loyalist, Jane Lane wondered, "What kind of woman can win here? Does it take Pamela Anderson with half a brain?" A scary image. Even scarier is that the O'Brien campaign, given its insistence on flogging the abortion issue down the stretch, didn't understand a basic truth grasped by both of these activist women. "Abortion just didn't catch on, because it wasn't an overriding issue," said Lane. Adds Marsh, "People don't vote on abortion, but Democrats make it their litmus test."

Why? Among Massachusetts boomer elites, issues surrounding abortion have "totemic status," notes Marsh. Allegiance to the full abortion rights agenda has "the power to generate money and elite support. It cleaves easily to class distinctions." And to generational schisms. Democrats had seized majority power on Beacon Hill for the first time in the late 1940s with staunch opposition to birth control as one of their key issues. That was Tip O'Neill's generation; he served as Speaker of the Massachusetts House from 1949 to 1952. Fifty years later, a critical mass of Massachusetts Democrats, encouraged by the collapse of conservative church influence over the social beliefs of boomer Catholics, have staked out the opposite turf. But unlike Tip, who managed never to let his views on the matter impede his coalition building, his boomer successors have made it a defining, black-and-white issue. For them, personal belief in expansive abortion rights is a political prerequisite; you're either part of the solution or part of the problem. For Shannon O'Brien, whatever her personal beliefs, it became of overriding strategic importance to appease the left on abortion. Even Mitt Romney, wary of the gender gap, put a conveniently moderate spin on his longtime pro-life convictions.

That was then. Now that he's free of the conventions of the bluest state, Romney is eagerly promoting his conservatism on abortion, spinning the tale—unheard of by the Boston media before he started peddling it on the stump—of his pro-life epiphany after hearing stem-cell researchers discuss farming embryos.

For that flagrantly expedient conversion, and for similar campaign-trail pandering to the right on stem-cell research and gay rights, Romney has been justifiably pilloried from across the political spectrum. (Conservative agitator Ann Coulter did him no favors when she told a conservative group that she admired the way Romney "tricked liberals into voting for him. I like a guy who hoodwinks the voters so easily.")

When he bows to the demands for conformity by right-wing pro-life zealots out on the stump, Romney must be reminded of home, where their generational peers insist on the opposite extreme. The pressure on politicians is hard to resist. Generational historians William Strauss and Neil Howe observe that the boomers are as likely to bend on personal issues such as abortion as they are to toss their Beatles records out with the trash. "As boomers begin entering midlife, a schism has emerged between . . . modernists and New Agers at one edge, and . . . traditionalists and evangelicals at the other," they write in *Generations.* "Each side refuses to compromise on matters of principle—believing . . . that 'it's just easier to have blanket absolutes.'"

As O'Brien and other aspiring female candidates in Massachusetts have learned, blanket absolutes may well be demanded of them by boomer activists, who then reward them with money and organizational support. But they're cold comfort after another losing Election Day. O'Brien's embrace of unchaperoned abortion rights for sixteen-year-old girls appalled older voters of both genders. But how to explain O'Brien's collapse among the younger women for whom abortion rights are by now a given? In a state where partisan enrollment has been in decline for decades and unenrolled voters are the majority, boomer absolutism on abortion has a partisan taint that some swing voters find offensive. In the 2006 gubernatorial election, abortion rights groups turned on Lt. Gov. Healey, a lifelong supporter of choice who had publicly clashed with Gov. Romney over his veto of access to emergency contraception. Her crime: declining to fill out extensive written questionnaires submitted by the National Organization for Women, the Planned Parenthood Advocacy Fund, and NARAL. Healey doubtless spoke for many politicians of both parties when she said she was just sick of filling out special-interest group questionnaires. "The lieutenant governor is pro-choice, and she has always been pro-choice," said a spokeswoman. "Until now, we have had no reason to doubt Kerry Healey's commitment to a woman's right to choose," agreed Melissa Kogut of NARAL, who could not cite any specific actions of Healey's that might betray a fraud. Still, she said, as the election season heats up, Healey "needs to clarify where she stands."

If the partisanship of liberal boomer absolutism on abortion doesn't turn off voters, the tone deafness of its proponents will. When the death of longtime incumbent Joe Moakley opened up the Ninth Congressional seat in 2001, it seemed a prime opportunity for Cheryl Jacques, an openly gay state senator who already represented a good chunk of the largely suburban district. Her main competition in a crowded Democratic primary was pro-life senator Stephen Lynch, a former ironworker from conservative, Catholic South Boston. With early funding from NARAL and other abortion rights groups, Jacques came at Lynch early and stridently on the issue. "He doesn't trust women," she bluntly told voters, who she claimed were "looking for someone who will protect women's rights." In one notable late-campaign moment, Jacques was speechless in front of TV cameras when asked if she would back a victorious Lynch in the final election against the Republican nominee, a pro-choice woman. In the end, significant numbers of pro-choice voters were eager to overlook their difference with Lynch on that issue and support his candidacy, conducted in a gentlemanly, low-key style reminiscent of Joe Moakley's. "I knew we had it when she came right out of the box screeching about abortion," a Lynch adviser told me after his man had won easily. "Rule number one is the first thing you talk about is how much you care about the seniors." Jack Duffy, chairman of the Wellesley Democratic Town Committee and a Jacques supporter, agreed that Lynch's focus on health care and education had proven more relevant to voters than his candidate's agenda. "If you ask the average suburban voter, 'What do you think of Cheryl Jacques?' they'll say she is a feminist candidate who has abortion on her mind," he said.

NARAL's Kogut and her peers see themselves as guardians of the temple of choice against Visigoths who want to roll back *Roe v. Wade,* and for them and their counterparts nationally, the battle feels forever engaged. But there hasn't been significant public support in Massachusetts for any retreat from abortion rights in many years. A string of relatively conservative Republicans have understood that and made a point of defusing the abortion brigades as best they can. William Weld and Paul Cellucci, who held the governor's office throughout the 1990s, simply outdid the Democrats in pledging allegiance to abortion rights, mollifying their moderate-to-conservative base with antitax, anticrime, and welfare reform policies. Mitt Romney acknowledged the public's support for choice by insisting he would do nothing to change existing state law, and by citing his mother Lenore Romney's pro-choice Republicanism as a personal inspiration. When abortion came up during the campaign, Romney would lower his voice and shake his head ruefully, visibly saddened by the very thought of abortion and the crass politicization of the issue by his opponent. But he didn't need to model an appalled reaction when Shannon O'Brien punctuated her absolutist position on parental consent with her unappealing tattoo-viewing invitation. The viewers at home, exit polls later showed, were horrified on their own.

As was Mary Anne Marsh. Although she told me she thought O'Brien had gotten a bum rap for her debate performance against Romney, and that she had at least answered the question honestly—in contrast to Romney's abortion dance—Marsh conceded that liberal ideological purity had blown it for the Democrats. "They would rather fall on their swords than win," she complained. "What I don't get is, why must the middle ground be ceded?"

But for the Massachusetts boomer liberal, the iconic personal value of abortion rights dogma overrides any pragmatic electoral goal. It blinds candidates, even veterans like Shannon O'Brien, to what really matters to voters, especially women. The great boom-era advance of females into the workforce—in blue-collar Massachusetts, at least, a movement fueled more by economic necessity than choice—had exacerbated a crack in the Democratic coalition. On one side of the gap were activist liberals with time to focus on a debate of little local importance; on the other were working women, mostly pro-choice, but with dozens of more pressing issues. Throughout campaigns, the activists act as key political gatekeepers within the Massachusetts Democratic Party, forcing their candidates to dance on a slippery seawall. Then on voting day, the workers have their say.

The end result is a natural phenomenon familiar to residents of Marsh's hometown. On Shelburne Road heading into Greenfield immediately after the Route 2 overpass is a "gravity hill" created by the natural obscuring of the horizon. From beneath the overpass, the road seems to rise slightly toward a distant crest. But there is no such incline. Thus, a car stuck in neutral at the "bottom" appears to slowly move uphill. Its progress is an optical illusion, as misleading as the political abortion obsession that denies its practitioners the power they claim to want most.

The failure of women to thrive in Massachusetts politics has many fathers—and mothers. Boomer women still must fight through the self-preservationism of an almost all-male status quo. Camelot wasn't known for its feminism, unless serial infidelity and exploitation are now feminist traits. In this heavily Catholic state, the church has not exactly modeled feminist behavior, nor has the liberal establishment. Todd Gitlin, the Harvard man who helped found Students for a Democratic Society, recalls how a painful gender gap split their New Left ranks when women "were the first to grasp . . . that the male-run movement was moving nothing but itself."

But what's killing the Democratic women in Massachusetts politics can't be blamed on the men. Too many progressive women here still stunt their political prospects by obsessive emphasis on their most cherished dogma. This habit does the national liberal cause no good. Sen. Hillary Clinton stepped on the third rail in mid-2006 with a speech deploring abortion as a "sad, even tragic choice" and advocating prevention of unwanted pregnancy through more access to contraception and reproductive health care. That was way too much sympathy for the devil for Melody Drnach, action vice president for the National Organization for Women. "I would like Senator Clinton, as I would like all pro-choice representatives, to start any conversation about reproductive justice and reproductive health by saying, 'I support access to safe, affordable, legal abortions,' period," she said. And God forgive, if she can, Hillary's betrayal in supporting pro-life but otherwise liberal Democrat Bob Casey in his successful run against incumbent U.S. senator Rick Santorum in Pennsylvania. "That is of significant concern to us," warns Drnach, whose group sent out a NOW PAC Alert predicting that the nomination of a pro-life Democrat would "result in sure defeat," and warning that "it will do women no good if both major parties are hostile to women candidates and women's rights."

Hillary Clinton's run for the presidency might seem an ultimate moment of validation for liberal boomer identity politics. The first woman to run. A key strategist in two winning presidential races that harnessed the power of the gender gap. A staunch supporter of expansive abortion rights succeeding a hard-line pro-lifer. Wouldn't even the most principled liberals—even those like Drnach and her sisters at NOW, who would balk at trading a far-right Neanderthal with a zero NARAL rating like Rick Santorum for a moderate like Bob Casey within a new Democratic majority—be down for that? Marie Wilson of the White House Project, a group devoted to electing a woman president, is skeptical. "Progressive women in particular want the first serious female candidate to be 100 percent perfect on issues," says Wilson.

One hundred percent perfect, like the reflections ideological purists see in the mirror. But there's a problem with flawless images of the imperfect. They're an optical illusion, like the "progress" of women up the gravity hill of Massachusetts politics. And for Mary Anne Marsh, the frustrating failure to move forward is a symptom of boomer selfishness. "There is a generational difference," she says. "My mother to this day doesn't use sugar, because you made sacrifices for the war effort, people did the right thing. You went to war, you got the GI bill when you returned, there was an honest exchange. You sacrificed for the common good, and in exchange you got the American dream. Now, even though we're at war again, no one outside of the military is asked to sacrifice and no one does. It's the baby boomers being free agents—everyone's out for themselves." By indulging self-defeating behavior like the squandering of opportunities for the political advancement of progressive women on the altar of abortion rights absolutism, "we have allowed Massachusetts to be the poster child for everything that's wrong with the Democratic party," she concludes. "If you really care about something, you have to be willing to accept less than a complete victory."

CHAPTER FIVE

....

Mistaken Identity

THE SECOND NIGHT of the 2004 Democratic National Convention was a moment of pure bliss for the Massachusetts political establishment. As they drifted in from the cocktail parties and hospitality suites and settled into their choice seats in the Fleet Center, Boston's first party convention ever was off to a good start. (The only minor annoyance: a Thanks for Nothing! Go Bush! sign bolted to the front of a pizza joint across from the arena that had been forced out of business for the week by convention security concerns.)

Former presidents Bill Clinton and Jimmy Carter had whipped up the crowd on opening night, a mere appetizer for what lay ahead. In forty-eight hours, John Kerry, one of their own, would officially receive the party's nomination for president, the second Massachusetts politician to win it in sixteen years and the fourth since 1980 to make a serious run at it. Even though the Clinton and Carter speeches were a reminder of how only two southerners had managed to interrupt the string of Republican presidencies over the past thirty-six years, George W. Bush's sagging poll numbers offered hope that Kerry could return Massachusetts Democratic influence to its rightful Washington address.

But for the boomer liberals who dominate the local Democratic elite, this was a night to pay homage to a key element of their political identity—the crusade for civil rights. Warm-up speakers included poet Maya Angelou and veteran congressman Bennie Thompson, the senior black elected official in Mississippi. Then, it was Senator Ted Kennedy's turn.

"I've waited a very, very long time to say this: Welcome to my hometown!" bellowed Ted. "To Americans everywhere whose aspirations have been kindled anew by this campaign we, who convene here tonight in liberty's cradle, say, Welcome home! Welcome home for the ideals born in Boston and strengthened by centuries of service and sacrifice. Ideals like freedom and equality and opportunity and fairness and common decency for all—ideals that all Americans yearn to reclaim." With many in the crowd waving Kennedy signs on cue, you could almost imagine yourself in the old Boston Garden on election eve 1960, watching John F. Kennedy speak to a spellbound crowd. That was a long time ago, the last time "Boston-born" ideals captivated the nation and voters yearned for a Massachusetts Democrat at the helm. Back in the good old days of Jack and Bobby, when, as Ted was recalling it for the delegates, "we fought for equality and justice, for civil rights and voting rights and the rights of women, for the cause of Americans with disabilities." A totality of oppressions. We are what a corrupt political system does to us; the personal is political.

Identity politics—that distinctive talisman of the liberal boomer—have been at the core of the Democratic Party's self-image ever since. But the way this political class interprets their generation's civil rights impulses has coincided with a rarely interrupted string of losses. Behind Ted as he spoke was one reason why. As a visual companion to podium rhetoric, the convention's TV-savvy planners had included special bleacher seats, visible in wide camera shots, stocked with a reminder of the civil rights revolution that followed JFK's election, a Noah's ark–ready array of citizens representing major ethnic and racial categories. One delegate wrote in her blog that a lucky bleacher-seat occupant she met had been instructed not to wear any bright clothing or jewelry that might distract from the effect, explaining, "She's meant to be a piece in the tapestry." At least she was spared the indignity suffered by delegates to both the Democratic and Republican national conventions in 1996, who were all but forced to repeatedly perform the Macarena for the cameras as a show of solidarity with Hispanic voters.

Photo-op diversity is nothing new across the bipartisan political spectrum of the boomer era. But for the Democrats it was essential to match the window dressing onstage with the party platform approved that very evening by the convention. The document noted the fortieth anniversary of the Civil Rights Act of 1964, and reaffirmed the Democratic vow that "all of our people should have the opportunity to fulfill all of their potential, and each of us should be as equal in the eyes of the law as we are in the eyes of God. That is the America we believe in. That is the America we are fighting for. That is the America we will build together." While the national party placed its civil rights rhetoric at the end of the white paper in deference to the timeliness of national-defense and economic issues, the Massachusetts Democratic platform made no such concession. It led off with a list of civil rights pledges, including support for "affirmative action initiatives," "American Indian tribal sovereignty," and "constitutional guarantees to all people regardless of gender, ethnicity, race, religion, age, income, national origin, disability, or sexual orientation." Massachusetts was the only state carried by the 1972 presidential campaign of George McGovern, a nominee made possible by the enshrinement of an array of quotas in the party's delegate selection process. Accordingly, Massachusetts Democratic by-laws require that the party's ruling committee include "two French-speaking members (one of each sex), two Portuguese-speaking members (one of each sex), five men and five women who are gay and lesbian Democrats, [and] two members representing the disabled (one of each sex)."

So it was with palpable self-satisfaction that the Massachusetts delegation, after sending Ted offstage with more Kennedy sign-waving, jumped to their feet again to greet the evening's featured attraction, the brightest black hope in the Democratic Party, Senate candidate Barack Obama of Illinois. Obama was only the second African American to deliver the convention's keynote address since Barbara Jordan did so, in 1976. His selection was emblematic of the party's determination to convert its fascination with identity politics from a Republican wedge issue into a political asset. Left-wing black party celebrities like Al Sharpton and Jesse Jackson—whose quadrennial convention addresses used to air in prime time—popped up in obscure early-evening slots, seen only by C-Span junkies.

American liberalism's black face this time around would not be a fire-breathing preacher with a sermon full of angry demands. Instead, as the crowd roared in approval, a dignified, light-skinned black man spoke compellingly about his love for America in Hallmark terms. Obama called the nation a "tolerant . . . magical place." In a stylistic nod to the Kennedys, he challenged his audience to "reaffirm our values and our commitments, to hold them against a hard reality and see how we are measuring up, to the legacy of our forebearers and the promise of future generations." And he brought down the house with an appeal for racial conciliation that seemed an explicit repudiation of identity politics: "There is not a liberal America and a conservative America—there is the United States of America. There is not a Black America and a White America and Latino America and Asian America—there's the United States of America."

Standing in a media skybox watching his speech electrify the hall, I couldn't help recalling the spring night in 1968 when James Brown and a white Irish mayor had taken to a now demolished stage a few yards away, the same platform that JFK used on election eve 1960, practicing what they preached about racial harmony and sparing Boston the agony of rioting after the King assassination. It wasn't a happy memory. It made me wonder whatever became of the long-ago promise of a new, biracial Massachusetts politics, and what exactly the local politicians in the loge seats heaping adulation on Obama that night—every last one of them as white as can be—had done to deliver on their vows of justice and equality for African Americans.

Pathetically thin though it may be, the anemic representation of women at the table of political power in Massachusetts is a windfall compared with black access. The most recent survey by the Joint Center for Political and Economic Studies ranked Massachusetts twenty-first among the fifty states in number of black elected officials. Our puny yield of sixty blacks serving at all levels of elective government is barely half that of Oklahoma, a state with a smaller black population. Incredibly, prior to the surprise victory of Deval Patrick in the 2006 gubernatorial race, it was Republicans who could make a better case for being the state's historic party of inclusion. Before the fall of 2006, only one black man had been elected to statewide or federal office, Edward Brooke, a Republican who served two terms in the U.S. Senate in the 1960s and 1970s. The highest-ranking elected black in Boston in recent times was Ralph Martin, the county district attorney during the 1990s—another Republican. Although several legislative districts have been gerrymandered over the years to create majority nonwhite districts, few blacks or Latinos have been elected to the legislature, and most of those who did have failed to move up in the ranks. The lone black state senator, a liberal Democrat, spent a good part of 1997 under house arrest for failing to file her federal tax returns.

The sparse litany of black success is a particular embarrassment to Massachusetts Democrats, considering the state's close identification with the civil rights movement. This was the home of abolitionism, the intellectual breeding ground of Ralph Waldo Emerson, William Lloyd Garrison, and W.E.B. DuBois. Massachusetts men underwrote John Brown's 1859 attempt to free the slaves at Harpers Ferry; a Massachusetts woman, Julia Ward Howe, wrote the lyrics that immortalized his role in the push for emancipation, sung to the tune of the "Battle Hymn of the Republic." A century later drum majors for justice from Massachusetts went south in droves to help with voter registration and organizing protests during the 1960s. The state was on the front lines again in the 1970s for backing court-ordered integration of the systematically segregated Boston public schools. Most recently, Massachusetts has poured billions into an education reform plan aimed at closing the racial achievement gap in the public schools.

Mission not even close to accomplished. One recent study found only 15 percent of African American fourth-graders in Massachusetts were rated proficient in reading. That's less than a third of white student proficiency, ranking us thirty-eighth out of the forty-two states with available data. According to research by www.civilrights.org, Massachusetts has the nation's eighteenth most segregated school system, with 25 percent of black students attending schools with more than 90 percent nonwhite enrollment. While black per-capita income here exceeds the national average, as does that of whites, there's still a huge gap between the races. In aging, increasingly hopeless Massachusetts cities like Springfield, black incomes trail the

national numbers. According to the 2000 census, only 31.6 percent of Massachusetts blacks own their own homes, less than
half the white rate, the sixth-worst record of any state. By
comparison, South Carolina and Mississippi lead the nation
with 61 percent, and most southern states boast black home-
ownership rates above 50 percent. Perhaps worst of all, African
Americans here continue to bear the brunt of our persistent violent crime problem, ranked the nation's seventeenth-worst by
the United Health Foundation.

How dangerous is it to be a poor or working-class black
resident of Massachusetts? The state's best known black activist, Rev. Eugene Rivers of Boston's Azusa Christian Community, felt right at home when he saw the 2002 movie *City of
God,* depicting rampant crime in a Rio de Janeiro slum. "We
got 58,000 millionaires here, and there are pockets in the most
liberal state in the union that look like something out of *City of
God,*" he says.

Rivers is a Harvard graduate who, unlike most of his college classmates, has firsthand knowledge of slum life. He was
raised in North Philadelphia, where he ran with a teenage
gang. As a Bostonian, he has been an eyewitness to the brazen
street violence that torments local blacks. In July 1990, gun-
shots ripped into his second-floor bedroom in the middle of
the night and through an interior wall, nearly clipping his
three-year-old son. Another two dozen rounds were emptied
into the blue Dodge van parked out front that Rivers used to
transport congregants of his storefront church. The strafing
was seen as a warning from local drug dealers to back off his
efforts to steer local kids away from the thug life through

church outreach. Rivers wasn't the only local preacher trying to fill the void of a black community in crisis but distrustful of the cops. But he was the first to organize both black and white clergy in a coherent way to lobby for grants, political support, and a better social safety net. "As young, well-educated African Americans we are called to a ministry that melds spiritual renewal with economic retooling and political struggle in the service of youth caught up in vicious street gangs," Rivers told an interviewer the summer his house was shot up. "To challenge young black people morally, we must help them to create jobs for themselves, equip them to renew their family lives and organize with them to call to account a power structure that does not serve their interests."

Take away the religious packaging, and Rivers might have passed for an updated version of the more sincere inner-city radicals of the 1960s, a social activist intent on salvaging his community without any unrealistic expectations of help from The Man. But the genius of Rivers's faith-based approach was his emphasis on morality and self-help, evocative of the Nation of Islam, but also appealing to a black community rooted in the church, white power brokers impressed with his entrepreneurship, and beleaguered working-class taxpayers tired of waiting to see results from their social spending. His networking with other clergy evolved into the Ten Point Coalition, a national model of faith-based social problem solving. During the 1990s, as Boston's murder rate plummeted, Rivers became a national celebrity, earning a *Newsweek* cover spread in 1998. The Clinton administration and local politicians basked in the success of the so-called Boston Miracle, a community-policing alliance between social-service agencies, law enforcement, and the preachers. For the Massachusetts Democratic establishment, the Miracle was a pleasantly validating surprise, proof that liberals could crack down on crime without turning the cops loose to crack skulls in the streets, the flowering of the seed fertilized in the triumphant James Brown concert after Dr. King's murder. Local pols waved off concerns from academic observers that the drop in crime was fueled more by a temporary demographic hiccup, a sharp decline in the numbers of young males likely to offend. "We know how to do this now," Massachusetts attorney general Tom Reilly told me after one pep rally for the Miracle attended by President Clinton. "We've found the answer."

But it turned out that the Miracle—like the love affair between Gene Rivers and the liberal establishment—had a short shelf life. Rivers was pugnacious and often politically incorrect. In late 1992, with Boston's poor black neighborhoods consumed by deadly gang wars over crack-dealing turf, Rivers shocked local academic elites with an angry open letter—"On the Responsibility of Intellectuals in the Age of Crack"— indicting them as clueless dilettantes. With an in-your-face flourish aimed at liberal self-righteousness, Rivers borrowed part of his title from a 1967 essay by left-wing icon Noam Chomsky of MIT that lambasted the liberal intelligentsia for failing to vigorously oppose the Vietnam War. "Chomsky's points now apply with particular force to the responsibility to tell the truth about the condition of the black poor," wrote Rivers. "Faced with the emergence of a nihilistic 'new jack' generation, ill-equipped to secure gainful employment even as productive slaves," the work of prominent black intellectuals such as Henry Louis Gates and Cornel West was little more than useless "piles of denunciation of all conceivable 'isms' and 'phobias.' . . . We are entangled in a web of inherited and unexamined ideological and political assumptions—for example, an incoherent conception of rights divorced from moral obligations. Living on borrowed assumptions, we now face moral and cultural obsolescence. In a tragically Proverbial sense, we are now elites bereft of relevance."

The bereft elites weren't pleased. Cornel West in particular took offense at the notion of a gap between his well-compensated academic lifestyle and the carnage in the streets of black America. He dismissed the idea that "you suffer from survivor's guilt if you are not organically linked with the black community. Take Eugene himself as an example—on the one hand one of the most brilliant intellectuals I have ever met; on the other hand full of anxieties about that." Rivers's alleged anxieties didn't constrain him from personally working the streets, making contact with young gang-bangers and lobbying for peace. Some local liberals were alarmed by Rivers's mixing of missionary tactics and religious belief with social doctrine, and said so. But he found support from the likes of the Boston Clergy Breakfast Group, including leaders of two dozen Protestant, Catholic, Jewish, Hindu, and Muslim communities who financed his early "street missionary" hires. And while some police were antagonistic, Boston's crack wars were bloody enough for black Deputy Supt. Willis Saunders Jr. to publicly welcome the help. "Rev. Rivers is a capable man who is interested in the community and doing the right thing, which is working with our youth," he said.

More than a decade later, as I sat with Rivers in his worn Victorian home in the Dorchester heart of Kennedy country, his frustration over the lack of change for the better was palpable. The dip in the crime-committing demographic was over, and the drug gangs were back in force. Rivers had moved his young family out of the sketchy neighborhood where his bedroom had been shot up, and into a worn Victorian in a leafy, middle-class black section of Dorchester. But once again, the war came home. In December 2005, punks with a beef invaded the basement hangout of Rivers's next-door neighbor's son and slaughtered the teen and three of his friends. While Rivers had become a major player in national faith-based activist circles, his latest local project—an effort to recruit an elite corps of off-duty cops and street workers, some of them ex-gang members, to stage tough-love interventions with at-risk kids—was struggling to find local funding.

Rivers had committed an unpardonable sin by becoming an early, high-profile supporter of the Bush administration's faith-based initiative allowing churches and explicitly religious groups unprecedented access to federal social-service grants. Rivers shared the attitude of the initiative's Democratic leader, University of Pennsylvania professor John DiIulio, that "I'm not in this administration because I feel like being a Republican [but] because I believe this is a way to get poor people and people in need the services they need." Just weeks after President Bush launched the program, Rivers was blunt enough in his public comments about a power struggle with white fundamentalists to draw the nickname "Johnnie Cochran with a clerical collar" from a leader of the archconservative Southern

Baptist Convention. But with the exception of Boston mayor Tom Menino, a wary but willing ally of Rivers, all that didn't seem to matter to the local liberal establishment. Rivers and the other local ministers in the Ten Point Coalition had pioneered a grassroots approach to social activism that seemed to some individuals suffering in American ghettoes like a dream from the 1960s come true. But here at home it was getting the cold shoulder.

"The fact that the entire country resonated to the intellectual and practical arguments of the faith-based initiative, and the folks who were least supportive of the entire model were here in Massachusetts, is just a deep irony," says Rivers from behind stacks of newspapers, books, grant-proposal forms, and letters piled high on his dining-room table. "The amazing thing is, I'm a Democrat. On any of a number of policy issues, I am to the left of most of my liberal friends. But none of the high liberals or academic intellectuals here have wanted anything to do with a functional role for faith in addressing these problems. I have been the skunk at the garden party." No wonder. National surveys suggest roughly 40 percent of Americans attend religious services weekly, compared with only about 20 percent of Massachusetts Democrats, according to statewide polling in late 2006. (Inside Route 128, the interstate highway that circles greater Boston and defines the home turf of most of the region's liberal elites, 58 percent admit they attend either "a few times a year" or "never.")

Nearly fifteen years removed from his challenge to local intellectuals to place meaningful social action ahead of identity-politics mau-mau, Rivers' expectations couldn't be any lower.

"There is a high paleoliberal intelligentsia that has been domi-
nant here, and they do not have a rudimentary comprehension
of American society, an understanding and respect for other
parts of the country." He laughs sarcastically at the memory of
the shock among his liberal acquaintances over anemic black
turnout for John Kerry in 2004 swing states where gay-rights
issues were on the ballot. "They were surprised that a very conservative, black-church-attending portion of the electorate was
not going to take well to pushing the same-sex marriage
agenda," Rivers says. Ironically, Kerry himself opposes gay
marriage but, in a repeat of the liberal abortion-rights litmus-
test syndrome, was forced to pander to its proponents throughout the campaign. Homage had to be paid to the trendiest of
all civil rights issues at the moment. In a conversation with one
of Kerry's biggest fund-raisers, Rivers noted the sea of white
faces atop the Kerry campaign hierarchy and asked him,
"When is John going to desegregate the leadership of his campaign?" The reply: "Our campaign has diversity. We've got a
gay guy."

On the inner-city crime issues he cares most about, Eugene
Rivers believes Massachusetts liberals, recoiling from the failure of boom-era social-welfare schemes and the attendant collapse of black urban culture, have long since looked the other
way, indulging in self-gratifying but useless identity babble instead of confronting black criminal reality. "The multicultural
discourse that celebrated difference was all university-based
political nonsense that had no political or policy utility on the
planet Earth," he sneers. "There was no appreciation on the part
of liberals that a macro-structural paradigm of oppression

didn't explain the violent behavior of black kids who would spend $200 on sneakers, refuse to go to high school, and mug a defenseless senior citizen in the black community. Anyone who talked about blacks and crime was a racist and was dismissed." And politically incorrect black activists who dared to point out boomer-liberal impotence in dealing with inner-city crime were an increasingly endangered species. In late 2006, Rivers found himself portrayed in thinly sourced articles in the local press as a "brutal" *Godfather*-like figure, willing to use violence against street kids who angered him, and as an eager tool of right-wingers hungry for a colorful Uncle Tom.

It was suddenly open season on Rivers in part because Massachusetts liberals had a new black action figure to play with. Like Rivers, Deval Patrick grew up poor in the ghetto and caught a series of breaks that landed him a Harvard education. But while Rivers headed to the streets to try to break up gun-wielding crack gangs, Patrick wound up defending gang-bangers as a specialist in death-penalty cases for the NAACP Legal Defense Fund. While Rivers was helping organize the Boston anticrime model and export it to other cities during the 1990s, Patrick spent three high-profile years as assistant attorney general for civil rights in the Clinton administration, prosecuting affirmative action cases so aggressively he earned the nickname "The Quota King" from his right-wing critics.

By 2005, flush with cash from several lucrative years as a high-profile lawyer for corporations such as Coke, Texaco, and predatory mortgage lender Ameriquest—fending off charges of civil rights violations—Patrick was ready for a new challenge. His entry into the 2006 race for governor of Massachusetts electrified local liberals. Unlike the impolite, Bible-quoting likes of Rivers and other Ten Point Coalition preachers, Patrick was an African American activist they could feel completely comfortable with. Light-skinned with well-tailored suits and an Ivy League syntax, Patrick quickly became the darling of the aging boomer activists and donors who occupied the liberal wing of the state Democratic party. His platform shied away from any serious, specific reforms—such as allowing more experimental, nonunion charter schools that might give young blacks the same airlift he had taken out of a failing ghetto school. Instead the platform hinted at more expansive social spending while decrying "dishonest" tax cuts. His stump speech was a feel-good spectacular right out of the Kennedy era, replete with positive buzz phrases about reaching out to "people who have checked out" to get them to "check back in." In a bow to Clinton's influence, Patrick's favorite campaign word was "hope." The campaign slogan was "Together We Can." The campaign song: "Proud" by Heather Small. ("What have you done today to make you feel proud?") Not what have you done today to help the poor, but "what have you done . . . to *make you feel proud*." In the final days of the primary race, following Patrick to "community meetings" packed with adoring fans, I saw eager boomers bring their grandkids to meet the candidate, some telling him "you remind me of Jack and Bobby." On cue, Patrick thrilled a primary-eve crowd with his reply to critics who claimed his campaign was mostly gauzy rhetoric with little substance. "We hold these truths to be self-evident, that all men are created equal. Just words? Ask not what your country can do for you. Just words? I have a dream.

Just words? Listen, I'm no Dr. King; let me say it before you do. But I do know that well-chosen words, spoken with conviction, can be a call to action.... What I'm talking about is what it takes to lead."

Evoking an era of youthful idealism, Patrick held a mirror up to aging boomer liberals and said of the reflection: See? You're still beautiful, and I am in your image. They responded by delivering both a sweeping primary victory over two long-time Democratic-party figures and a landslide win in November. But less than three weeks into the general election race against Republican Lt. Gov. Healey, this boomer Love Boat hit an iceberg that might have sunk it in any other state.

Years earlier, Patrick had written fawning letters to, and raised legal defense funds for, a convicted rapist, Benjamin La-Guer, a dark-skinned Hispanic whose case had been a cause célèbre in local legal circles due to questions of racism tainting the jury. Patrick joined the choir of prominent local figures demanding a new trial for LaGuer—a conclusion he later admitted he had come to without ever reviewing the case files or contacting prosecutors—but backed off when a controversial DNA test appeared to confirm LaGuer's guilt. Still, the Healey campaign pounced on his refusal to repudiate earlier statements that he found LaGuer to be "thoughtful and humane." Asked one Healey ad, "What kind of person continually defends a brutal rapist?"

As polls showed the flap eating into Patrick's big lead, his supporters, baffled and furious, cried racism. "A modern-day lynching?" asked one post to a local pro-Patrick blog, Blue Mass Group. Sympathetic columnists and editorialists were prevailed upon to add to the finger-wagging. Then Patrick got lucky. The *Boston Herald* ran an ugly story about how Patrick's brother-in-law, convicted of raping his wife thirteen years before but since reconciled with the candidate's sister and living in the Boston area, had failed to register as a sex offender as required by state law. Later that day, a visibly furious Patrick read a statement to reporters: "My sister and her husband went through a difficult time, and through hard work and prayer, they repaired their relationship and their lives. Now they and their children—who knew nothing of this—have had their family history laid out on the pages of a newspaper. Why? For no other reason than that they had the bad luck to have a relative who is running for governor. It's pathetic and it's wrong. By no rules of common decency should their private struggles become a public issue. But this is the politics of Kerry Healey. It disgusts me. And it must be stopped."

The Healey campaign denied any connection with the story, but the backfire burned hot. Healey's already high negative ratings soared. Polling late in the campaign confirmed that crime was a "very" or "moderately" important issue to 91 percent of the electorate, especially so for lower-income and minority voters. But boomer voters liked Deval Patrick's style and the idea of electing a black man. While early-fall surveys showed Healey's views on crime far more popular than Patrick's, at the end of the campaign far more voters somehow found Patrick tougher on crime than his opponent. The personal appeal of Patrick's candidacy had trumped its political weaknesses.

As Patrick prepared to take office in early 2007 amid a mounting body count in the mean streets of Boston and other cities across the state, there was little evidence of any emphasis on crime in the governor-elect's portfolio. The topic drew only one vague, passing reference in his lengthy election-night victory speech; none of the nineteen members of his transition committee had an obvious public safety link. An academic opinion survey of minorities that fall had found 37 percent of blacks citing crime as the most important issue facing the state; only 4 percent of whites concurred. At this moment of triumph for identity politics, of sublime exculpation of liberal Massachusetts's deplorable record on racial empowerment, creative and aggressive action on the one issue most damaging to the state's blue-collar communities of color seemed as unlikely as ever.

All of which draws a sarcastic laugh from Gene Rivers. "The moral and intellectual hypocrisy of the Massachusetts liberal is that on the one hand, you want to say you are friend to the black and poor, but you don't want to be held responsible for the terrible conditions," he says. "And more disturbing than the actual conditions themselves is their refusal to ask the question: how is it their left-liberal ideology permits or tolerates such intolerable conditions? How does that happen in Kennedy country?"

CHAPTER SIX

....

Blaming America First

WHY DO THE working-class voters of Massachusetts keep sending Ted Kennedy back to the Senate, wonder appalled out-of-state conservatives? The last surviving Kennedy brother may be best known around the country as the poster boy for big-government liberalism's hypocrisies and excesses, the boozy playboy who failed to promptly report the 1969 car accident in which a young woman drowned and still had the nerve to make an incoherent, mercifully failed run for president in 1980. But at home, Ted is more often seen as the undisputed champion of vital state economic interests in Washington. "He is the best quarterback for cities and towns, and his staff is the best offensive line in Washington," says a lobbyist for Massachusetts municipal governments. Kennedy is "a one-person economic engine for the state" when it comes to federal funds for research, health care, and public works projects, adds Michael

Widmer of the business-funded Massachusetts Taxpayers Foundation. Ted's national image may still be that of "a doctrinaire liberal, a spokesman . . . for a cause whose time is gone," as Adam Clymer puts it in his definitive bio of Kennedy's Senate career. But in Massachusetts, where seniors sometimes must choose between prescriptions or heat and where multiple jobs aren't always enough for low-wage workers to get by, Ted's agenda doesn't seem dated at all. When a president talks about health care or the minimum wage during a State of the Union address, "who do they show in the cutaway on TV?" asks one local Republican activist who has tried futilely to unseat Ted in the past. "He's been coming up with a wealth of proposals, one after another, that you could easily make a case for and carry."

Mitt Romney's 1994 run against Ted was the toughest reelection fight Ted has ever had in Massachusetts, and there will likely never be another one remotely as challenging. Beyond his stature as the state's Beltway godfather, Kennedy has in his old age achieved almost mythic status as a symbol of stoic endurance. In December 1999, Bill Clinton was the headline speaker at a nationally televised memorial service for six firefighters from Worcester, a blue-collar central Massachusetts city, who had perished in an awful warehouse fire. But it was Ted who delivered the most memorable eulogy, an eloquent allusion to his own personal losses that came just months after the death of John F. Kennedy Jr. in a plane crash. "I wish that loved ones did not have to die too young," he said. "I wish that tragedy never haunted a single soul. But I know that sometimes life breaks your heart."

Beyond the right-wing chorus that blames activist government for everything up to and including head lice, few here hold

Ted accountable for liberalism's domestic policy failures. But foreign affairs—the chronic Achilles heel of the modern-day Democratic Party—is a different story. As Peter Beinart notes in his plea for a more muscular liberal foreign policy, Ted is far removed from the relative hawkishness of his older brothers. By 1984, Beinart writes, the aggressively anticommunist "cold war liberal establishment was gone. The holdovers from that earlier age—men like [1984 Democratic nominee Walter] Mondale, Ted Kennedy, and House Speaker Tip O'Neill [D-Mass.] had long ago internalized the cultural liberalism and foreign policy dovishness" of the first wave of boomer liberals, 'McGovern's children.'"

Kennedy didn't start out that way. Early in his public career, young Ted parroted JFK's aggressive Red-bashing, warning of Soviet aggression in Germany in a 1961 speech reminiscent of George W. Bush's rationale for "staying the course" in Iraq: "The fall of Berlin could be a prelude to the fall of Boston." But freed of the constraining influence of his older brother, Ted became a high-profile leader in the Democratic Party's leftward drift on foreign affairs, arguably dating back to one of his first major crusades on behalf of the 1965 Hart-Cellar Act, the landmark liberalization of U.S. immigration laws. Said Ted at the time, in a spectacular display of nonprescience: "The bill will not flood our cities with immigrants. It will not upset the ethnic mix of our society. It will not relax the standards of admission. It will not cause American workers to lose their jobs."

Originally a strong supporter of his brother's and Lyndon Johnson's escalation of the U.S. presence in Vietnam, by 1969, picking up where the murdered Bobby Kennedy had left off,

Ted had turned sharply against the war. In the years that followed, he became a critic of U.S. foreign policy in Latin America, a backer of lifting the trade embargo with Cuba, and a supporter of the nuclear freeze movement. Over the years, Ted has evolved into one of the Senate's most reliable voices against U.S. military intervention, scoring a 97 percent rating in a 2005 *National Journal* ranking of liberalism on foreign policy.

Ted's antiwar instincts have long-standing historical precedent in Massachusetts political culture. During the Mexican-American War of the 1840s, Boston-based abolitionist William Lloyd Garrison's newspaper *The Liberator* openly supported the Mexican cause. "Every lover of Freedom and humanity throughout the world must wish them the most triumphant success," it editorialized. Perhaps the most famous demonstration against that war came from Henry David Thoreau, who was jailed for refusing to pay the state poll tax in protest. The incident prompted Thoreau to write the essay, "Civil Disobedience," which provides a Rosetta stone for the modern-day boomer's conviction that the personal is political. "Must the citizen ever for a moment, or in the least degree, resign his conscience to the legislator?" Thoreau asked. "The only obligation which I have a right to assume is to do at any time what I think right."

More than a century later, Massachusetts was again a center of antiwar activism, this time against the formative foreign-policy issue of the boom generation, the Vietnam War. A local peace activist, Jerome Grossman, conceived the 1969 National Moratorium Day protests that cemented the mass-movement credentials of the antiwar protesters. John Kerry became the best known leader of Vietnam Veterans against the War.

Rejecting the rally-'round-the-flag notions taken for granted by their parents' generation and reflected in John F. Kennedy's vow to "pay any price, bear any burden, meet any hardship, support any friend, oppose any foe, in order to assure the survival and the success of liberty," boomers made Thoreau's philosophy their own. They updated it into "Vietnam syndrome," the conviction that U.S. military intervention is to be avoided at all costs and, ideally, never attempted.

Its philosophical merits aside, the practice of placing personal convictions at the core of complex foreign-policy decisions is a legacy that's been crippling the political prospects of liberal Democrats for more than two decades. In a famous speech to the 1984 Republican National Convention, UN ambassador Jeane Kirkpatrick, mocking the leftward tilt of the Democratic Convention that year in San Francisco, coined a phrase that the right still employs to bludgeon liberals. "When the Soviet Union walked out of arms control negotiations, and refused even to discuss the issues, the San Francisco Democrats didn't blame Soviet intransigence. They blamed the United States. But then, they always blame America first. When Marxist dictators shoot their way to power in Central America, the San Francisco Democrats don't blame the guerrillas and their Soviet allies, they blame United States policies of 100 years ago. But then, they always blame America first."

Unfortunately for Democratic efforts to shed that caricature in the post-9/11 environment, the impulse still thrives in Massachusetts. On a cold, rainy day just before Thanksgiving 2005, I drove to a working-class neighborhood in Quincy, a blue-collar community known as the "City of Presidents" for being the birthplace of John Adams and his son John Quincy Adams. The Adamses were foreign-policy hawks. But on this day in their old hometown, the doves were ascendant.

Gathered behind a bank of microphones were current and former boomer figures from the state's all-Democrat congressional delegation. They had come to join in what amounted to a campaign event for Venezuelan president Hugo Chavez, the virulently anti-Semitic communist strongman who had risen to power amid international concerns over vote fraud and suppression of dissent. With a Venezuelan TV crew broadcasting the proceedings back home live, representatives of the Chavez government beamed as Ed Markey, Quincy congressman Bill Delahunt, and former congressman Joe Kennedy, Ted's nephew and Bobby's eldest son, delivered discounted home-heating oil shipped to Massachusetts by CITGO, the Venezuelan state-owned oil company.

With a banner featuring the Venezuelan flag behind them, the Massachusetts politicians took turns praising Chavez as a humanitarian and bashing Bush as oblivious to the home-heating needs of the working class. "What our president has done is turn a blind eye to what our real problem is," said Markey. Delahunt offered "a profound thank you" to Chavez and CITGO, whose "willingness to assist low-income citizens here in Massachusetts truly demonstrates what good corporate citizenship is all about." Added Kennedy, "Here you have a country that is being led by someone who cares about the poor."

When I questioned Kennedy later, he acknowledged that the CITGO shipment "will not even come close to meeting the needs of low-income people that are applying for help this

year." But that's nothing new for Chavez, whose anti-U.S. rhetoric may thrill the blame-America-firsters of the Massachusetts
liberal elite, but does little to assuage the suffering of the
Venezuelans, half of whom earn less than $2 a day. Despite vast
oil wealth, Venezuelan poverty has held constant since Chavez's
election in 1998, according to researchers at the Andres Bello
Catholic University in Caracas. Only 10 percent of the workforce has jobs; the rest scuffle for a living in the "freelance"
economy. Amid the poverty, violence thrives; 90 percent of the
estimated twelve thousand people murdered each year are men
between the ages of fifteen and thirty-five. As *New York Post*
columnist Douglas Montero found when he visited the slums of
Caracas shortly after Chavez's headline-making visit to the
UN, the climate of fear snuffs out hope for the likes of Manuel
Gonzalez, a teenager who can't take advantage of his only shot
at an education because his mother is afraid to let him out to attend night school. "A 15-year-old who wants to work and be a
productive member of society hasn't even started school yet?"
wrote Montero. "Hugo, who's the devil now?"

All this was irrelevant to Kennedy, Markey, and Delahunt.
In their Massachusetts social and political circles, alliances with
U.S. antagonists—at least, when they're being antagonistic toward a Republican administration—are intuitively understood
to be in line with Thoreau's dictum of following one's "conscience." For Markey, his lead role in the nuclear-freeze movement of the 1980s had felt like the right thing, the moral thing,
to do. It turned out later that the deployment of nuclear missiles
in Western Europe helped lead to the collapse of the Soviet
Union and the end of the cold war. But that historical lesson

didn't stop Markey from reviving the idea after September 11, proclaiming that "the Bush administration is leading the country in the wrong direction in almost every aspect of nuclear policy." Joe Kennedy's foreign-policy portfolio includes staunch support of former Haitian president Jean-Bertrand Aristide, whose return to power Kennedy celebrated in a 2001 op-ed column. "Some critics call Aristide a threat," he wrote. "I have found him to be an honorable man who looks out for the poor and the vulnerable." That fantasy had collapsed by 2003, when a *Los Angeles Times* report found Aristide's rule to be "a chronicle of dashed expectations" resulting in the deterioration of Haiti from a poverty-stricken disaster area to "an even poorer wreck of a nation gripped by hunger, hopelessness, disease and gang warfare," with the highest rate of HIV and AIDS outside sub-Saharan Africa and the world's third most corrupt society. Not present that November day in Quincy, but surely there in spirit, were two other Massachusetts congressmen active in foreign affairs: Jim McGovern of Worcester, one of the left's most consistent critics of U.S. policy toward Cuba and Barney Frank of Newton, who once filed a federal trade–policy reform bill that, said one analyst in horror, "would allow the state of Massachusetts to set American trade, defense and foreign policy."

And for Bill Delahunt, the Quincy pep rally was merely the latest event in a long-standing relationship with Chavez, whom he calls "an excellent friend." Beginning in 2002, Delahunt hosted a series of meetings at Massachusetts resort areas of the Grupo de Boston, including Chavez administration officials and members of the Venezuelan opposition. According to one news account, "participants often engaged in heated political talks in the mornings (one session needed an intervention to stop a fistfight). They also went whale watching and played intramural baseball. Bottles of scotch were in the guest rooms, and all had been consumed by the end of the session." Chavez partisans praised the sessions; his critics dismiss them as worthless charades that provided a fig leaf for Chavez's suppression of political dissent. "I don't work for Condoleezza Rice" was Delahunt's response to suggestions that he was undermining U.S. policy toward Chavez. "I don't report to the State Department. I report to the people who elected me in the state of Massachusetts."

Voters here don't seem to mind. Delahunt, Markey and company are part of an experienced congressional delegation— headed by Ted Kennedy, an acknowledged master of the inside game in Congress—that over the years has harvested an impressive array of federal spending for Massachusetts. But the reflexive affinity of Massachusetts liberals for anti-U.S. regimes and rhetoric has ramifications beyond the state's borders. The success of the 2005 Quincy publicity stunt clearly emboldened Hugo Chavez, who made a September 2006 visit to New York that disrupted the Democratic Party congressional election strategy. In a speech to the United Nations, Chavez denounced Bush as "the devil himself," waved a copy of a Noam Chomsky book about "America's quest for global dominance," and said of the podium where the U.S. president had spoken the day before, "It smells of sulfur still today." The next day, Chavez spoke at an event in Harlem staged to highlight yet another donation of heating oil. He ridiculed President Bush as "an alcoholic, a sick man with a complex." He praised Castro and saber-rattling Iranian president Mahmoud Ahmadinejad. And he accused the U.S. military of staging the September 11 attack on New York City: "To take planes filled with passengers and smash them into the twin towers, that's barbarism."

Leading Democrats, already nervous about softening poll numbers in the wake of the fifth anniversary of September 11, were appalled, and rushed to denounce Chavez's statements. "Despicable and disgusting," said Sen. Chuck Schumer, head of the Democratic Senatorial Campaign Committee. "Hugo Chavez abused the privilege he had, speaking at the United Nations," said House Democratic leader Nancy Pelosi. "He is an everyday thug." And Rep. Charles Rangel, a New York Democrat and as much an admirer of Castro and other leftist leaders as anyone in the Massachusetts delegation, was quick to pile on. "George Bush is the president of the United States and represents the entire country," said Rangel. "Any demeaning public attack against him is an attack on all of us."

None of this bothered Joe Kennedy, who ran TV ads during the winter of 2007 touting the Chavez oil shipments. And to Bill Delahunt, secure in his Massachusetts cocoon, Chavez's rantings were, while stylistically "inappropriate," speaking truth to power. "For him to be able to say that puts into context in what low esteem the United States is held, not just in the Islamic world, but all over," he said. This assessment fits neatly into the paradigm that boomer liberals have constructed in the bluest state. Their instinctive generational contempt for U.S. military interventionism is a fundamental character trait. Thus, Vietnam syndrome is a chronic form of civil disobedience as Thoreau envisioned it, the calling to place one's personal "conscience" above any alleged "obligation" to the national interest, however debatable that might be. The more this disobedience conforms with the "low esteem" in which countries—their own wretched records of social and economic justice notwithstanding—hold America, the bigger the boost to the self-esteem of the boomer.

Delahunt and friends have learned well from their role model. On May 6, 2002, Ted Kennedy awarded the annual Profile in Courage Awards, given to public servants who "follow their conscience" by taking "principled stands for unpopular positions." Among the recipients that day was Kofi Annan, the UN secretary-general, by then six years into a disastrous tenure that included the pillaging of the Iraq oil-for-food program; the failure of peacekeeping operations in Bosnia, Haiti, Liberia, Rwanda, and Somalia; and the overall deterioration of the UN's international clout and prestige. But Annan had become a vocal critic of the Bush administration's response to September 11 and, accordingly, a target for criticism from the right. That was enough for Ted to give Annan the award named for his brother's Pulitzer Prize–winning book that honored such notable nonpacifists as John Quincy Adams and Sam Houston. He "has risked the wrath of world powers and many other countries to do what he believes is right," said Kennedy. "In Kofi Annan we have a dynamic profile in courage who is meeting the challenge of this generation."

This Kennedy country conceit—that courage and righteousness in foreign affairs are the near-exclusive province of America's detractors—may be the bluest state's most damaging export of all. Barack Obama writes of being repulsed by conversations with his college classmates during the 1970s that "slipped into cant [at] the point at which the denunciation of capitalism or American imperialism came too easily." In mid-2006, a widely circulated article by LA songwriter Seth Swirsky cited the Massachusetts attitude as cause for abandoning the Democrats. "I used to be a liberal," wrote Swirsky, who found himself in 2004 "still fantasizing that Democrats would constitute a party of truly progressive social thinkers with tough backbones who would reappear after 9/11." But after watching leading Democrats react to world events since then—such as when "Senator Kennedy equated the unfortunate but small incident at Abu Ghraib with Saddam's 40-year record of mass murder, rape rooms and mass graves, saying 'Saddam's torture chambers have reopened under new management, U.S. management' "— Swirsky concluded that "I was wrong. The left got nuttier, more extreme, less contributory to the public debate, more obsessed with their nemesis Bush—and it drove me further away."

In December 2006, confirmation of Swirsky's observation was provided by the premier chat room of the Massachusetts liberal, the letters to the editor page of the *Boston Globe*. Four readers responded to an op-ed piece by Latin American scholar Ana Julia Jatar denouncing Chavez as a totalitarian fraud and appealing to American liberals to remember their "legacy of opposing right-wing, authoritarian regimes throughout Latin America. They should not stain that legacy by embracing the authoritarian Chavez simply because he comes from the left and joins them in fighting President Bush," Jatar wrote. Two correspondents endorsed Jatar's take. "Chavez's rhetoric is an insult to and the antithesis of the liberal ideals of liberty and social justice," wrote Maria Antonini. Bill Delahunt and Ted Kennedy "remind me of the well-intentioned folk who used to return from the Soviet Union filled with stories of all the wonderful things Stalin was doing for his people," added Robert Bottome. But to Jeff Duritz, Jatar's argument simply "repeats a shrill cry from Venezuela's former ruling class." And the Rev. Mike Clark dug deep into the boomer bag of 1960s maxims when he predicted that Chavez's reelection would be proof that "he offers an alternative to those whom history has overlooked. It could be an opportunity for all of us to ask ourselves which side we are on." More interesting than the debate, however, were the addresses of the debaters. Clark and Duritz wrote in from Watertown and Somerville, two archliberal enclaves that abut Cambridge. Antonini and Bottome submitted their politically incorrect views from a bit closer to the scene of Chavez's glorious revolution—Caracas.

What now? Distaste for the war in Iraq more than matched fear of terrorism on voting day in 2006. For Massachusetts Democrats like Ted Kennedy, who was calling Iraq "George Bush's Vietnam" early on, vindication is sweet, and will likely fuel the blame-America-first reflex. But that instinct can easily leave Democrats in a politically treacherous corner. In late 2005, the congressional debate over re-authorization of the Patriot Act was roiled by reports of the Bush administration's warrantless wiretaps on overseas phone calls. Ted Kennedy wrote an outraged op-ed piece in the *Boston Globe* that climaxed with the frightening story, then ricocheting around the Internet, of a Massachusetts college student being visited by two government agents simply because he had tried to borrow a copy of the *Communist Manifesto* from the library. "Think of the chilling effect on free speech and academic freedom when a government agent shows up at your home—after you request a book from the library," wrote Kennedy. "Incredibly, we are now in an era where reading a controversial book may be evidence of a link to terrorists."

One little problem—the student soon admitted his story was a hoax. A minor embarrassment to Ted, who need never worry about re-election. But his eagerness to repeat virtually any criticism of U.S. policy is a reflex that has had dire political consequences for Democrats before. Will it do so again? It's the same political choice so often bungled by abortion-rights absolutists. What are the political consequences of that instinct should there be another successful terror attack on U.S. soil between now and election day that suddenly throws the party's emboldened antiwar wing on the defensive? Is the role of antiwar backlash in the 2006 election gains really a call for more of the Massachusetts-style Americaphobia that so alienates voters who might otherwise be easy Democratic pickings? And is it really worth risking a reversal of the 2006 gains to find out?

CHAPTER SEVEN

Windsurfing to Oblivion

BY EARLY 2003, after a lifetime of wanting a presidential run, John Forbes Kerry—JFK for short—was ready to rumble. After seeing his name floated as a possible contender in 2000, he had run unopposed for reelection to the Senate in 2002. Kerry's new Web site, www.johnkerry.com, was up featuring photos documenting his Purple Heart, Bronze Star, and Purple Star–winning tour of duty in Vietnam. He was even brushing up on his Spanish, the better to bond with Latino voters. And unlike 2000, the timing seemed right for Kerry to go for the big one. As a decorated veteran and longtime member of the Senate Foreign Relations Committee, Kerry was a sought-after Democratic voice on issues relating to the war on terror on the network newscasts and TV talk shows. With Al Gore out of the mix, who could bring more suitable credentials to the 2004 campaign than Kerry? Sen. John Edwards of

North Carolina? Too green. Rep. Richard Gephardt of Missouri? Where is *his* Purple Heart?

Kerry's role model John F. Kennedy had bluntly confronted communism in Berlin, Cuba, and Vietnam. In his inaugural address, John Kennedy had exhorted the rising boom generation to "pay any price, bear any burden, meet any hardship, support any friend, oppose any foe, in order to assure the survival and the success of liberty." As a matter of policy, this was not exactly what Kerry had in mind. His father, Richard, a veteran U.S. Foreign Service officer, was a blame-America-firster, quitting the Kennedy administration in disgust over its anticommunist rhetoric, and later writing a book indicting America for the "fatal error" of propagating democracy and heeding "the siren's song of promoting human rights." But while Kerry the younger was an avid student of his father's ideology, Kennedy's contemporary macho appealed to him as it did to so many young boomers. JFK had *Profiles in Courage* to run on. Kerry had both color videos of himself in action in Vietnam and countless hours of news footage of his leadership in the antiwar movement—*Profiles in Courage* squared. Just in time for the first post–September 11 campaign, he had cemented those credentials by supporting the invasion of Iraq on the Senate floor in a speech that notably repudiated Vietnam syndrome.

"I know for [fellow Vietnam veterans] Senator [Chuck] Hagel, Senator McCain, and myself, when we pick up the newspapers and read about the residuals of the Vietnam war, there is a particular sensitivity because I do not think any of us feel a residual with respect to the choices we are making now," said Kerry. "I know for myself back in that period of time, even as I protested the war, I wrote that if my nation was again threatened and Americans made the decision we needed to defend ourselves, I would be among the first to put on a uniform again and go and do that." And Kerry had concluded that moment was at hand. "It would be naive to the point of grave danger not to believe that, left to his own devices, Saddam Hussein will provoke, misjudge, or stumble into a future, more dangerous confrontation with the civilized world. The threat of Saddam Hussein with weapons of mass destruction is real."

This was not the time to invoke Vietnam, Kerry explained: "We are living in an age where the dangers are different and they require a different response, different thinking, and different approaches than we have applied in the past." Just as his generation had in their twenties spread the word of the war's futility and immorality, it was again time for boomers—preferably a Yale alum not named Bush—to explain a hard truth, that this war was the opposite.

In Massachusetts, antiwar liberals were stunned by Kerry's vote. Some picketed his Boston office. Randall Forsberg, head of the pacifist Institute for Defense and Disarmament Studies, drew 20,000 votes as a last-minute write-in candidate against Kerry. Wellesley College political science Professor Marion Just saw a cross-generational union taking form. "There is a youthful antiwar movement who have the hippie generation to wake up with, and they are alarmed at how quickly we appear headed to war," she said.

But Kerry was unfazed. He had quoted John Kennedy in his Senate speech: "The cost of freedom is always high, but Americans have always paid it. And one path we shall never choose . . . is the path of surrender, or submission." His past voting record on authorizing the use of force may have had more hairpin turns than the Pacific Coast Highway: a vote against a Republican president's battle plans on the eve of the 1991 Gulf War ("There is a rush to war here"), then support for retaliatory attacks on Saddam in 1996 under President Clinton ("It is far better as we've all learned through experience to meet the challenge up front, early, right away"). But in the wake of the mass murders in Manhattan, Pennsylvania and Washington, he felt politically secure in this latest zag. Vietnam, he explained in an interview days after his vote, had been "a very different time and war, our country had not been attacked." The mostly aging-boomer protesters outside his office left Kerry "a little puzzled," he told me. What had been so clearly the right thing for Kerry to do back in the early 1970s was just as clearly a misguided objection to his equally righteous course of action now. "Having protested a war, I'm sympathetic to people's right to do it, but I don't understand people who disagree with what we have to do," Kerry said.

A few weeks later, preparing to host a TV roundtable discussion of Kerry's presidential prospects, I read his famous 1971 testimony before the Senate Foreign Relations Committee, the celebrated, career-making speech in which he wondered: "How do you ask a man to be the last man to die in Vietnam? How do you ask a man to be the last man to die for a mistake?" Kerry led off his remarks that day by recounting the testimony he had heard—and obviously believed—from Vietnam veterans at an event publicizing atrocities allegedly committed by U.S. troops "on a day-to-day basis with the full awareness of officers at all levels of command." Kerry recounted their stories of having "personally raped, cut off ears, cut off heads, taped wires from portable telephones to human genitals and turned up the power, cut off limbs, blown up bodies, randomly shot at civilians, razed villages in a fashion reminiscent of Ghengis Khan, shot cattle and dogs for fun, poisoned food stocks, and generally ravaged the countryside." Continuation of the war, Kerry charged, was "the height of criminal hypocrisy." And he issued a sweeping indictment of an older generation's willingness to risk lives in pursuit of what he termed purely face-saving political goals: "Where are the leaders of our country? Where is the leadership?"

After the TV taping, I asked one of the guests, a former Kerry staffer and longtime political ally, if Kerry's testimony might come back to haunt his presidential campaign. How would his emphasis on U.S. military "war crimes" sit among revenge-seeking voters with little post-9/11 patience for Vietnam syndrome? And couldn't Kerry's long-ago charges of politically expedient hypocrisy on the part of Washington power brokers be hung on him now by the inheritors of his antiwar reflex? She thought about it for a second, then shook her head. "It won't be a problem," she concluded, "because everything he said back then was right."

To those who still wonder why Kerry's 2004 presidential campaign so grossly underestimated the impact of the Swift Boat Veterans for Truth ads attacking him as "unfit"—including one ad consisting entirely of the aggrieved reactions of fellow vets to that 1971 Senate testimony—there is your answer. Kerry is a product of a Massachusetts political culture that, in the boomer era, has little tolerance for the conflation of patriotism and military strength that is standard in most of the rest of the nation. Of the more than one million U.S. military personnel stationed in the United States or its territories, only 2500 are located in Massachusetts, the ninth-fewest in the country, fewer than tiny Rhode Island. In one 2003 study, Massachusetts had the nation's lowest proportion of military recruits to eligible population. Massachusetts colleges were among the first to ban military recruitment on campus during the Vietnam War era. That tradition continues in the hands of the likes of Rene Gonzalez, the University of Massachusetts graduate student who touched off a national uproar after the widely publicized death of former pro football player Pat Tillman on active duty in Afghanistan, by writing in the college paper that Tillman was a "pendejo" (idiot) who "got what was coming to him."

During the course of Kerry's thirty-five-year political career in this antiwar bell jar, the details of his time in Vietnam and his antiwar activism upon returning had rarely been seriously questioned. Instead, they served as his chief political credential, a powerful profile in courage that persuaded scores of followers to overlook his aloof demeanor and self-serving political behavior. In his first Senate campaign, a Democratic primary opponent trying to outflank Kerry on the left, Jim Shannon, claimed that if he had truly opposed the Vietnam War, "you would not have gone," a charge Kerry turned into gold by accusing his rival of impugning "the service of veterans in that war by saying they are somehow dopes or wrong for going." That strategy proved to be a wise, fence-straddling choice for Kerry, who swamped Shannon among more conservative blue-collar voters, while assuring liberals that he had the stature to carry the antiwar fight in Washington. "If elected, Kerry would be the only Democrat in the Senate to have served in Vietnam," noted the *Boston Globe* editorial page approvingly, even though they had endorsed Shannon in the primary. "That credential would be vital in a Senate debate over the wisdom of sending troops to Nicaragua." Twenty years later, the author of that editorial, Martin Nolan, was still confident of Kerry's military bona fides. "The Bush campaign longs for a McGovern-Mondale-Dukakis rerun, hoping the Democratic foe is weak or passive," he wrote. "Kerry has made mistakes and has yet to articulate what his priorities as president would be, but like another Massachusetts liberal with the initials JFK, war and combat are not metaphors to him. He is strong and aggressive."

But instead of a compelling, all-American figure capable of exploiting the unimpressive military credentials of fellow boomer George W. Bush, Kerry's ace card was easily trumped during the campaign. The Democratic National Convention, a week-long celebration of Kerry's military service, failed to significantly improve his standing in the polls. The word was already out about the distinguishing characteristic of Kerry's foreign-policy record: politically expedient ambivalence. In voting against authorization for the first Gulf War in 1991, Kerry had dismissed the notion that such a vote represented only a first step toward a military response, arguing instead that Congress would have "no further say." A dozen years later, he defended his green light for the war in Iraq by saying it was simply an authorization to threaten Saddam Hussein.

Most notoriously, Kerry tried to have it both ways on his 2003 vote against $87 billion in supplemental funding for U.S. forces in Afghanistan and Iraq, explaining that "I actually did vote for the $87 billion before I voted against it." Bush operatives could scarcely believe their good fortune. "Senator Kerry voted against benefits for our troops who were in combat, voted against providing them with the body armor they needed, voted against providing armor for the Humvees. And now he's saying that he's for those things and the president is the one that's against them," said Bush campaign manager Ken Mehlman in a 2004 interview touting a new attack ad on the subject. "What you have is someone who has a reality that he wants to hide from. And so the campaign has created this parallel universe where he attacks on the very things that he's vulnerable on."

A "parallel universe"—an apt description of life for John Kerry inside the Massachusetts political cocoon. During his first two terms in the Senate, Kerry became known as the least responsive member of a congressional delegation that generally prided itself on constituent service. "You call and call, and nobody even calls you back," one municipal official told me of his efforts to get Kerry's help dealing with a federal agency. "I have to tell my whole story again every time to each snotty kid who picks up the phone." With workhorses like Ted Kennedy in the Senate and Joe Moakley in the House, organizations, businesses, and individuals needing help with federal issues learned to simply bypass Kerry's operation. But this neglect became a sore point during Kerry's toughest reelection challenge, his 1996 race against Massachusetts governor William Weld, when a large group of local Democratic officeholders cited Kerry's unresponsiveness as their main reason for endorsing the Republican.

Kerry started returning phone calls for a while after that, but only for a while. In 1999, I staged a test of political responsiveness in which an intern wrote letters to all of her elected representatives, from city councilor up to governor and U.S. senator, asking for a response on an issue within their purview. Some replied more quickly than others. Only one politician failed to respond at all. Kerry's explanation: "We get five thousand pieces of mail a week and our staffs have been cut back." Two years later, we tried the same test again. Again, Kerry finished last, his office even failing to return follow-up calls placed by my intern after waiting a month for a reply. And again, Kerry tried to blame it on a high volume of mail and on staff cuts imposed by GOP Senate leaders. Informed that other members of the congressional delegation with fewer office resources had performed far better, he bristled. "It is our highest priority, trust me, we have an extraordinary record," he snapped. "Sometimes out of thousands of letters, one may slip through the cracks. I can show you letters from people who say you're the only office that ever got back to us."

The arrogance and evasiveness of that answer are familiar to local veteran Kerry watchers, who recall the revelation that in 1991, his income tax return showed zero charitable donations from his six-figure income. Kerry first tried to pass it off as a clerical error. "I was so pressed to get my return in on time, I was here in Boston, the receipts that I had were in Washington, and so I just put in a zero not thinking that people were gonna try to, you know, interpret this somehow," he told me at the time. Under further questioning, a different spin emerged. "I'm not in a position to be able to give more; I'd like to be able to give more; some years I was able to give more, but in 1991 particularly, I had some very serious expenses for my children, medical and otherwise, and I just wasn't able to do it." No explanation was ever given for his behavior in 1993, when he could afford only $175 out of his $126,000 salary for charity, far less than the 3.1 percent of total income the average American donates annually, but found $8,600 to buy himself a fancy Ducati motorcycle from Italy.

"The imported motorcycle, that was classic Kerry," says Charley Manning, a veteran GOP activist and consultant to some of the handful of Republican boomers who have won statewide elections in Massachusetts. His experience with Kerry goes back to 1984, when Manning worked for the campaign of Ray Shamie, a local businessman who ran for the open Senate seat that year. Shamie, a self-made millionaire, had run a competent race against Ted Kennedy two years earlier. He was likeable, optimistic, Reaganesque in a year when Reagan even carried Massachusetts. And he was giving Kerry, a dour figure after his nasty primary battle with Jim Shannon, a run for it when the *Boston Globe* dropped a bomb on him. The paper somehow got hold of old Shamie campaign memos worrying about the fallout should it become known that Shamie had briefly been a member of the rabidly anticommunist John Birch Society a decade before. They were right to worry. The *Globe* hammered Shamie, declaring the Birch Society "crypto-fascist" and portraying Shamie as the front for "an updated, computerized mass-mailing systematic organization of hatreds known as 'the New Right.'" A mere fifteen years after Ted Kennedy's lost weekend on Chappaquiddick Island, the paper editorialized that Shamie's "grandfatherly image masks a character not in keeping with the tradition of senators from Massachusetts." To hammer the point home, retiring Sen. Paul Tsongas announced that the notion of Shamie taking his seat was "obscene."

The Shamie campaign fought back with jabs at Kerry's Vietnam-era activism, but that didn't sell in a political culture where early-wave boomers who defined themselves by the intensity of their antiwar sentiment were in control. General George S. Patton III, son of the World War II commander, had to be dumped as honorary chairman of Veterans for Shamie after he claimed Kerry's work with Vietnam Veterans against the War had emboldened the enemy and led to military deaths in the battlefield. "There's no soap ever been invented that can wash that blood off his hands," Patton had said, to the derision of the local political establishment. A similar backlash took place when questions about Kerry's battlefield conduct were raised during his 1996 reelection fight with then governor William Weld. David Warsh, a *Boston Globe* columnist and former Vietnam War reporter, was derided for a column he wrote speculating on whether Kerry had committed a war crime by executing a wounded Viet Cong during combat. Kerry pulled rank in that exchange, too, castigating Warsh as a wartime "desk jockey."

In Massachusetts, the Vietnam card has been a lifetime passport to promotion for Kerry, who liberals saw as the perfect combination of antiwar activist and decorated war hero, acceptable to both blame-America-firsters and that curious swath of the blue-collar populace that equated military service with patriotism. Kerry pulled way ahead after the Vietnam-Birch exchanges and beat Ray Shamie by ten points. To Charley Manning, a tall, cheerful product of a Kennedy Democrat Irish-Catholic upbringing, the circumstances of Kerry's victory were a precursor to his collapse against Bush twenty years later. "In his own mind, he had been able to slide by because the press here is pretty liberal and he could basically get away with anything he wanted to," says Manning. It stunned most locals, he points out, to learn during the 2004 race that Kerry had been an altar boy; the senator had never felt the need to advertise his Catholicism before going national. "It doesn't fit into the model up here," notes Manning. "That would be seen as very uncool. The Democratic Party here is so secular, no one would ever think of talking about their faith."

As a lead dog in the boomer vanguard of the bluest state, Kerry could enjoy an enviable run in the upper echelon of power without much accountability for his contrivances and excesses, both political and cultural. Most of Kerry's anger over the 2004 Swift Boat veterans' attacks were directed at their challenges to the circumstances under which his war medals were earned. But Manning says it was common knowledge within Republican circles that "the ad that killed Kerry in state after state was that video of him [testifying before the Senate in 1971] in the phony camouflage, listing all the atrocities that Americans had committed in Vietnam. There weren't too many patriotic Americans who didn't see that ad and recoil.

The Bush people had that same ad ready, but once the Swifties did it, they didn't need it." And Manning says he was pleasantly appalled to see Kerry, supposedly armed with new wisdom about fending off "swift-boating" after his 2004 nightmare, scheduling a major antiwar speech in 2006 on the anniversary of his Vietnam atrocities testimony. Even the usually levelheaded Barack Obama still doesn't get it, writing in *The Audacity of Hope* of "the shocking efficiency with which a few well-placed ads and the chants of the conservative media could transform a decorated Vietnam war hero into a weak-kneed appeaser." Observes Manning, "To him and his friends, it's a celebration of his greatest accomplishment. To everyone else, it's a reminder of what was his absolute downfall."

For all of his laborious efforts to generate national political appeal, this distorted frame of reference has left John Kerry a stunted figure, afflicted with a form of political autism, unable to genuinely connect with outsiders. Protected from serious challenge by incumbency and a local political culture whose received wisdoms match his own, his indifference to local issues masked by Ted Kennedy's diligent constituent service, Kerry has been a prototype of the spoiled boomer, free to indulge his narcissism at every turn. This distinctive generational trait has had disastrous political consequences away from the Massachusetts cocoon. During a 2003 campaign stop at a famous South Philadelphia cheesesteak joint, Kerry offended the locals by declining the traditional mix of steak and Cheez Whiz, insisting instead on Swiss cheese. "It will doom his candidacy," predicted one local newspaper food critic. "In Philadelphia [Swiss cheese on a cheesesteak] is an alternative lifestyle."

As it turned out, Kerry barely won Pennsylvania, 51–49, well behind Al Gore's 5-point spread in 2000.

More profoundly, John Kerry's personality has often been publicly expressed through vague, self-indulgent orations that resemble the dorm-room monologues of a college-age stoner. In a fawning 1998 profile in *American Windsurfer* magazine ("A Windsurfer in the White House?"), Kerry told his interviewer that the pastime gave him "a great sense of meditation. . . . Spirituality is a fundamental for us. I think the more we learn about the universe, the more we learn about black holes and the expansion of the universe and the more we learn what we don't know about: our beginnings and not just of us, but the universe itself, the more I find that people believe in this supreme being. I'm a Catholic and I practice but at the same time I have an open-mindedness to many other expressions of spirituality that come through different religions."

That closing note of ambivalence will be painfully familiar to Kerry watchers. Aides to his 2004 campaign have acknowledged they were stunned to see the candidate taking to his windsurfing board with the presidency on the line. Set aside the alien status of the sport in the landlocked flyover states where the election was to be decided. The Kerry campaign was already struggling to fend off the crippling charge that he was a political weather vane, lacking principles that could stand up to a mild gust. Disastrously, Kerry's bucolic ride in Nantucket Harbor during the Republican National Convention was captured by news cameras and quickly turned into a devastating ad by the Bush campaign. To the tune of Strauss's "Blue Danube," Kerry glides back and forth while a narrator intones: "Kerry voted for the Iraq war, opposed it, supported it, and now opposes it again. He bragged about voting for the $87 billion to support our troops before he voted against it. He voted for education reform and now opposes it. He claims he's against increasing Medicare premiums but voted five times to do so. John Kerry: whichever way the wind blows."

"I thought it so perfectly conveyed the message," said senior Bush adviser Mark McKinnon. Yet Kerry might have overcome the windsurfing symbolism had his efforts to convey cultural empathy with lesser regions and lower classes not been so grotesquely forced. Few candidates could survive the unintentional hilarity of Kerry's awkwardly staged hunting trip in Ohio during the late stages of the 2004 race, when he strode into a grocery store and affected rural syntax as he asked, "Can I get me a hunting license here?" As he posed for photographers in his camouflage, Kerry hid a bloodstain on his hand, and refused to pose with the bird he shot, for fear of offending the antihunting crowd, or the merely squeamish.

Whichever way the wind blows. Voters here were as likely to buy that spin as they would the sound of George W. Bush extolling diplomatic nuance in fluent French. Massachusetts liberalism thrives in its own soil. But again and again during the boom era, its appeal has proven foreign to the national electorate. Kerry's attributes—intelligence, experience, and personal courage—are so buried under layers of ego, elitism, and self-indulgence, they are invisible to too many voters. It surprised no one who knows the full Kerry story that he humiliated himself and the Democratic Party in the final week of the 2006 campaign with his dated, unfunny joke about Bush's academic inferiority having gotten us "stuck in Iraq." For Kerry, the narrow 2004 loss to someone he considers his intellectual inferior (even though Bush had a slightly better grade point average at Yale than he did) was personal, a continuing source of smoldering fury to be stoked and vented even when all others have shifted focus to the future. His preference for Swiss cheese over Cheez Whiz? A matter of personal taste to be indulged despite the obvious political consequences and the poor etiquette of dictating changes in a well-known local custom. Bill Clinton famously abandoned his habit of taking a summer vacation on Martha's Vineyard when pollster Dick Morris determined a camping trip in Wyoming would be more helpful to his 1996 reelection campaign. But Kerry had to have his bout of personal communion with his windsurfing board, even if it needlessly invited predictable, election-jeopardizing consequences that put everything he purported to stand for at risk. It's a question of priorities, a word boomers often spell with a capital *I*. After all, there's a phrase that fits Kerry's initials, one hung on him by one of the many disgruntled Massachusetts Democrats left disappointed by his narcissistic behavior over the years: Just for Kerry.

CHAPTER EIGHT

······································

Cattle Rancher Among
the Vegetarians

I'M SITTING IN the kitchen of Mitt Romney's spacious home on a hill overlooking Boston, craving a beer that my tee-totaling host seems disinclined to offer, watching the impossibly handsome Romney lead his impossibly attractive family through a Diet Vanilla Coke taste test with improbable glee, and wondering, what's wrong with this picture? This is, after all, notoriously hard-drinking Massachusetts, where the sharp-elbowed popular culture couldn't be further from the *Ozzie and Harriett*–like scene in the Romney manse, where the diet cola is flowing freely as the governor romps on the rug with his grandson before Saturday-night family dinner. "Our favorite thing is being with the kids," Romney confides to me. "Having dinner and sitting around talking—that's what we love to do best." It's a typical scene in the life of a devout Mormon who, in accordance with church teachings, doesn't drink, smoke, or eat red meat, thereby rejecting three-fourths of the daily diet of the typical Bostonian. But Romney is not without his vices. Unlike his father, the late Michigan governor and GOP presidential candidate George Romney, who notoriously went to bed at 9:30 P.M. sharp every night, Mitt routinely stays up until 11, indulging in his version of a sinful before-bed ritual: eating a large "Jethro bowl" of sugar-laden cereal (albeit with skim milk).

Diabetic alert! While this close encounter with the Cleavers occurred at the start of Romney's term in office, the ensuing four years did little to alter that first impression. The most risqué comment of the Romney era came at a press conference announcing the elevation of his deputy corrections commissioner to the top spot. "I know it's not easy being number two," Romney remarked in front of incredulous reporters. "There are many days in this job when I feel like number two." As the governor giggled and flushed at the sheer scandalousness of his quip, I wondered anew about something I'd been puzzling over since that night of diet cola madness at Chez Romney: how did this guy ever get past the border patrol?

It wasn't for lack of effort to stop him. When Romney reentered the Massachusetts political arena in 2002 to run for governor, the Democratic establishment didn't just gear up for the challenge. In a classic case study of the narrow-mindedness and instinct for polarization that characterizes boomer politics, the Democrats tried to have him thrown out of the stadium before the game even began.

Shortly after Romney announced his candidacy, state Democratic Party officials challenged his status as a legal resident of Massachusetts. They claimed he had become an inhabitant of Utah during the three years he spent there salvaging the 2002 Winter Olympics from corruption and mismanagement. At a hearing before the state Ballot Law Commission that dominated the early days of the race for governor, Democratic lawyers portrayed Romney as a carpetbagger and a fraud, faking Massachusetts roots while living in his natural Mormon habitat. "Like many corporate CEOs, Mr. Romney refuses to accept responsibility for his financial behavior, for making false statements," said Democratic Party general counsel James Roosevelt Jr.

During the widely publicized hearing, the commission learned that Romney had maintained his Massachusetts bank accounts, voter registration, and seats on the boards of local civic institutions, returning often to his Belmont home for holidays and family celebrations, and otherwise fulfilling even the strictest legal standard of residency. This did little to curb Democratic charges that Romney had casually lied on official documents, a smear that drew an emotional statement from the candidate on the witness stand. "It really makes me feel sick, to tell you the truth," Romney said, appearing overcome. "There's nothing more important to me than my reputation for integrity. I inherited a great reputation from my mother and father, and I plan on giving one to my kids." Polls immediately thereafter showed Romney's popularity soaring, a trend that continued after the commission threw out the challenge, ruling unanimously that he had "never severed his ties to Massachusetts."

Romney was in the middle of one of a string of campaign photo-op "workdays" on a farm in western Massachusetts when word came of his vindication. "I am more determined to have the opportunity to serve the people that I love and the state that I love," he said, enveloped by the sweet smell of cow dung. "People do not want to hear about tricks to get me off the ballot. It's politics as usual, and I think people in Massachusetts are just tired of the old-style politics, the fear and smear, the attacks." Some leading Democrats publicly acknowledged that their party had handed Romney a public relations windfall, while making themselves appear narrow and petty. "That was the first of many mistakes," said John Barrett, the Democratic mayor of North Adams, after voters desperate for relief from the state's downward economic spiral elected Romney in November. "It set the tone, a bad one, of attack, attack, attack."

That Massachusetts liberals would reflexively resort to scorched-earth rejectionism didn't come as a surprise. Back in 1994 when Romney, a fixture on the Boston business scene for more than two decades but politically unknown, had challenged Ted Kennedy, his Mormon faith had been used to identify him as an unwanted alien. The Kennedy campaign put out the word, through Ted's boomer nephew Joe, that Romney was "a member of the white boys' club," a reference to the church's pre-1978 exclusion of blacks from the priesthood. Romney pointed out the irony of the tactic coming from the same family that so eloquently lobbied against anti-Catholic bias during JFK's run for president. The slur was retracted, but not before Romney's numbers took a hit. This time around, voters were more familiar and comfortable with both Romney and his religion; outside of the occasional heckler wanting to know where Romney's "other wives" were, the issue was never explicitly raised. But even before the residency challenge, Massachusetts Democrats again tried to demonize Romney as an outlier. At their party convention, O'Brien's introductory video opened with footage of snow-tipped mountains and gushing rivers. "This is Utah, land of majestic beauty," boomed the narrator. "It seems like a nice place. Let's send Mitt Romney back."

For a political culture that rhetorically extols diversity, it was quite the display of xenophobia. And over the next four years, Romney discovered just how insular and exclusionary the Massachusetts political culture is. "That whole 'you're not from here' thing flows less from a Massachusetts-centric view than from an ethnic and cultural view," Romney told me in late 2006 in an interview in the governor's office overlooking Boston Common and a statue of Mary Dyer, who was hanged on the Common in 1660 for the crime of being a Quaker. "I grew up in the Detroit area, and my friends came from a wide range of backgrounds. I didn't know what their ethnic background was. It never crossed my mind whether someone was Eastern European, Italian, or Irish. But when I came to Boston I learned that those distinctions were very important in this town. For me it was, 'He's not Irish, he's not Italian, he's something else—he's Mormon.'"

In part, this may be vestigial payback for the years when the immigrant ancestors of today's boomer Irish and Italians suffered from brazen Yankee discrimination. But it also evokes the predilection of boomer elites for stark polarization, the bipartisan engine of the blue vs. red schism in modern American politics. And in its especially bitter and personalized Massachusetts incarnation, this pack instinct had a huge impact on

Romney's governorship, with the well-being of working-class citizens as collateral damage.

Despite a massive budget deficit and pressing economic problems that required urgent attention, Mitt Romney's ability to function was hampered from the start by aspects of the legislature's political culture. For instance, House Speaker Sal DiMasi and Senate President Robert Travaglini were proud Italian Americans living in heavily Italian neighborhoods; much of the legislature was either Italian or Irish American. But, according to Romney himself and his top aides, two of Romney's brightest initial appointees, Jewish budget chief Eric Kriss and legislative liaison Cindy Gillespie, a southerner with a broad accent, found it difficult to establish comfortable working relationships with the Democrats. The going got noticeably easier when Kriss was succeeded by Italian American Tom Trimarco, and Gillespie gave way to an Irish Catholic aide named Peter Flaherty. "They like them, they trust them, they allow them to be critical," Romney says of the relationship between top legislators and the new staffers. And of the allegedly progressive political culture that fosters ethnic bonding, Romney observes, "Think of what it means if you're Hispanic or African American, how exclusionary that has to feel."

If the Romney-in-Massachusetts story ended there, it might be written off as a northeastern version of Mormon-dominated, staunchly Republican Utah, just another example of what happens when one culture rules an entire state. But it's also a cautionary tale of the damage done to regular people and the public interest when a reactionary political culture rejects des-

perately needed progress and reform out of vanity, defensive-
ness of the status quo, and sheer contempt for different social
and ideological perspectives.

Days after Romney's December 2005 announcement that he
would not seek a second term in office, Brian Mooney of the
Boston Globe—the liberal daily that served as the Bible of anti-
Romney sentiment—offered an assessment of the governor's
performance. "The broad reform agenda he promised in the
early days has been reduced by the political reality of Beacon Hill to a more modest series of legislative accomplish-
ments. Horse-trading and patronage, long the currency of
the State House, have been anathema to Romney. That reluctance to deal, combined with his uncompromising nature,
has meant that many Romney proposals—even bottom-line,
money-saving moves—were ignored, killed, or gutted by
the Democrats who run the Legislature. Close courthouses?
Not in our districts. Merge the Highway Department and
Turnpike Authority? Forget it."

Massachusetts political history is replete with stories of outsiders clashing with an entrenched power structure, often with
considerable success. In the early twentieth century, often corrupt ward bosses had a stranglehold on Boston until a coalition
of upper- and middle-class Yankees, Irish Catholics, and Jews
put sweeping charter reform on the ballot. It passed thanks to
strong support in key blue-collar ethnic districts. But nearly a
century later, a generation of virtual one-party rule has cemented a new breed of bosses into power on Beacon Hill.
These boomer kingpins couldn't be more stylistically different
from the James Michael Curley caricatures of *The Last Hurrah,*

but the currency they deal in—public contracts, patronage jobs, judgeships, and fattened pensions—is the same. A case can be made that the damage they do to the working classes in squandered tax dollars, foreclosed opportunities, and even physical endangerment outstrips their forebears.

In Massachusetts, these modern-day "rascal kings" come disguised as boomer lawyers, eager to mold the general laws to their liking and prevent pushy outsiders from doing the same. Long after most states had lowered the legal standard for proof of drunken driving to a blood alcohol content of .08 percent, a similar proposal couldn't get past first base on Beacon Hill. No one familiar with the state legislature was surprised. Roughly one-third of the legislators hold law degrees, the highest percentage in the nation and double the national average. An estimated three-fourths of them practice law outside of their legislative duties. The proximity of the statehouse to busy county and federal courthouses makes the double-dip logistically easy to pull off. And to the legions of bereaved survivors of victims of drunken drivers, many of whom have found that the state's lax DUI laws are easy to beat, this poses an apparent conflict with the public interest. Despite the Romney administration's emphasis on anti-drunk-driving legislation, it took a sustained, high-profile lobbying effort by Ron Bersani, the grandfather of a teenage girl struck and killed as she walked along a suburban road in 2003, to finally win passage of a long-awaited toughening of state penalties for repeat offenders. "I often wonder if they ever worry that one of the repeat offenders they help put back on the roads will some day kill one of their loved ones," Bersani wrote in an emotional appeal for passage of the law named after his dead granddaughter. "Probably not. After all, this always happens to someone else's family."

Meanwhile, the choicest spoils of the state's justice system—lifetime judgeships and cushy clerk-magistrate sinecures—remain all in the boomer-legislator family. In 2001, all five of the judicial nominees recommended by the powerful Democratic Speaker of the House were nominated and confirmed. So Beacon Hill Democrats were amazed when Romney stood by a campaign pledge to keep politics out of the judicial nomination process. In sharp contrast with accepted Beacon Hill practice, *Globe* reporting found "no partisan or philosophical pattern in Romney's judicial and clerk-magistrate nominations. Two-thirds were either Democrats or unenrolled voters who made political contributions to Democrats. Romney opposes marriage or civil unions for same-sex couples, but two of his thirty-six nominees were gay lawyers and advocates of rights for same-sex couples." In fact, while an occasional Romney campaign supporter found his way onto a minor board or commission, when it came to those plum courthouse jobs, traditional patronage requests "can be the kiss of death, according to a prominent politician who refrained from recommending a candidate for a judgeship because he feared it would hurt more than help," the *Globe* found. "I said what my rules were going to be," recalls Romney. "I wanted to get patronage out of the judicial system, but this is a very different culture. Where I came from in the Midwest, that's considered unethical and wrong. But in the Massachusetts culture, that's appropriate. People take care of their own."

James Michael Curley would understand. But the heirs of

his featherbedding tactics, in true boomer style, took it to an insufferable new level, circling the wagons around the inept Republican in charge of what's been called "the most scandal-prone waste of tax dollars in American history."

Watching the Big Dig—the massive, complex underground reconstruction of Boston's downtown highway and tunnel system—begin to take shape in the early 1990s, Romney shared the skepticism that led Ronald Reagan to futilely veto the project's funding in 1987. "You're gonna put a whole expressway below ground and keep another roadway system above ground in a city built on landfill?" Romney remembers thinking. "The whole concept struck me as not making a whole lot of sense." By the time he ran for governor in 2002, project costs for what locals nicknamed "the Big Pig" had soared from their original estimates by nearly 500 percent. Outraged out-of-state members of Congress had cut off federal funding, leaving Massachusetts taxpayers holding the bag for a financial burden that was drying up resources for badly needed local transportation and infrastructure improvements. And Romney was skeptical of the ability of Turnpike Authority managers to get the job done. "To have insiders managing it, political people, hiring friends and covering up mistakes—it's just doomed," Romney said.

So Romney made a campaign promise: he would press for elimination of the quasi-independent Massachusetts Turnpike Authority (MTA), the agency overseeing the Big Dig, and for transfer of control over the project to the executive branch. That struck a chord with voters already cynical about the cronyism and waste enveloping the Big Dig, but not with the

Democratic legislature, which had come to rely on the MTA as an employment agency for the politically connected. They booed the State of the State speech when Mitt Romney criticized lavish salaries for menial turnpike jobs, including highly paid toll takers, and the $450,000 price tag on a VIP celebration of a Big Dig tunnel opening (complete with performances by Keith Lockhart and the Boston Pops Esplanade Orchestra). When an opening on the turnpike board threatened to tip the balance of power there to Romney, the legislature quickly passed a bill adding new seats and empowering their cronies at the authority. "It's a haven for political friends and hacks, the last great seeding ground for patronage," said Romney. He recalls one top legislative leader's anguished question to a gubernatorial aide after Romney began his push for Big Dig control: "Who will take care of my people?"

It took the death of a Boston mother in the partial collapse of a poorly designed, ineptly installed roof of a Big Dig tunnel, six months from the end of Romney's term, to finally prompt the resignation of MTA chairman Matt Amorello and put Mitt Romney in charge. But that tragic stalemate was no mere by-product of typical partisan turf war. Amorello, the hapless Big Dig overseer, was a Republican, appointed to his post by Republican governor Jane Swift, his former colleague in the Senate.

That a Democratic majority would rally around Republican management of a project that was doing such palpable damage to the state's finances and ability to expand mass transit came as no surprise to Eric Fehrnstrom, Romney's director of communications and a twenty-year veteran at the statehouse as a newspaper reporter and political operative. "The party differences up here are far less important than whether or not you're an insider," he told me in an interview during the final days of Romney's term. "There are two political parties, the insider party and the outsider party, and you can find Republicans and Democrats in each of them." Romney came in as "a complete outsider" raised by his father, the late Michigan governor George Romney, to pursue and expect bipartisan collaboration. Over family dinner on the night of the big Diet Vanilla Coke showdown, Romney made it clear—naively, as it turned out—that he expected the public interest to trump personal and partisan friction. Restoring balance to the hemorrhaging state budget and reforming the hidebound political culture "is going to make me unpopular," he said. "But I don't worry about being liked. People respected my dad but didn't necessarily like him. The most important thing in life is not being liked. The most important thing is being true to who you really are."

Those assumptions worked for George Romney, who won acclaim in Michigan for his bipartisan initiatives. But this was boomer Massachusetts. The nativist attack of the residency challenge was just an appetizer. "Politics here is very personal, and I think that's an element that surprised the governor," admits Fehrnstrom. "He came in with the best of intentions, never took a salary, and never planned on making a career out of being governor." Massachusetts Democrats had grown used to Republican governors who talked a big game about reform during campaign season, then quickly lapsed into comfortable, conciliatory go-along-to-get-along mode. Bill Weld, elected on a reformist platform in 1990, quickly became so chummy with a leading symbol of tax-and-spend patronage politics, Senate President William Bulger, that he actually campaigned for Bulger against a Republican challenger, later appointing him president of the state college system. Weld's successors, Paul Cellucci and Jane Swift, were former state senators with impeccable insider credentials, and were even less inclined than Weld to criticize the status quo. But even before his inauguration, Romney made it clear his campaign promises were more than expedient posturing. Told that Bulger was balking at appearing before a congressional committee probing the activities of his serial-killer brother, James "Whitey" Bulger, second only to Osama bin Laden on the FBI's most wanted list, Romney was horrified. "It would be inappropriate for any citizen, let alone the president of a great university, to be in contempt of Congress," he told reporters.

Press accounts of Romney's comment noted how unprecedented it was for a politician of either party to take on Bulger over his relationship with Whitey, despite evidence that the "good" Bulger brother had long been his mobster sibling's protecter and confidant. Whitey was no Robin Hood; by the time Romney had the temerity to insist that William Bulger comply with a congressional subpoena, the public record was stocked with ghastly details of Whitey and his gang's rape and slaughter of innocents, including the especially charming penchant his henchmen had for driving through all-black neighborhoods of Kennedy country taking target practice on pedestrians. And the Democratic establishment's eagerness to defend William Bulger, like their protectiveness of the Big Dig's

Amorello, was especially peculiar given his stature as, by Massachusetts standards, an archconservative on social issues: he was pro-life, opposed busing to achieve school desegregation, resisted equal rights for gays and lesbians, and advocated education reforms bitterly opposed by the teacher unions.

"I don't owe anything to anyone," Romney told me over that preinaugural dinner. "I'd rather not be governor if I have to sign on to things I don't believe in." But while this bravado evoked boomer idealism, it proved to be crippling for Romney's agenda. Romney insisted he didn't have anything personal against either Amorello or Bulger, but the Democrats took his criticism of them as a personal insult, a gratuitous public indictment of their own clubbiness and hypocrisy, especially galling because the public sided emphatically with Romney. "Because Mitt wouldn't back down from his point of view, it earned him a lot of enmity from some of the insiders up here; it colored the way they reacted to the governor on other issues," says Fehrnstrom. "A lot of it has to do with how personal the politics are here. Mitt tried to depersonalize things, but I think in the way he governed he may have personalized the situation by taking on creatures beloved by the political culture here." It's a perception confirmed by Democrat Tom Finneran, House Speaker during Romney's first two years in office, which ended with a failed attempt to elect more Republicans to the legislature. That effort, predicted Finneran, "will sit with some as a debt that has to be repaid. The membership perceives Romney as being aligned with the business community, so they become hostile to that community. Some members look askance at that and say, gee, we need revenue, and why would we countenance a continuation of [pro-business] policy? So they go after the policy, and in the end what you reap is the loss of good jobs and hundreds of millions in revenue."

In a grim echo of modern-day Washington's infamous partisan gridlock, it's hard to find a controversial public-policy issue in Massachusetts during the era of boomer control that has been resolved by sheer force of goodwill and commitment to the public interest. In the most heavily hyped contemporary "example" of Massachusetts "bipartisanship," Romney was joined by top legislative Democrats and Ted Kennedy in the spring of 2006 at a grandiose signing ceremony for the state's universal health-insurance plan. Even though this complex measure is loaded with wishful thinking about consumer behavior, potentially backbreaking costs, and myriad other problems, its key architects immediately hit the road to tout their "breakthrough" to business groups, physicians, and other legislatures. Nothing was said about how little the new plan does to contain costs or seal the emergency walk-in care loopholes through which taxpayer dollars hemorrhage. "I do think people look to see cooperation from both parties and are tired of 'gotcha' politics," boasts Romney on the stump. "They are looking for people to help solve problems rather than just point out failures, and I'm proud that my legislature here was able to collaborate on something and make a huge difference." Even Sen. Hillary Clinton has joined the cheering squad. "To come up with a bipartisan plan in this polarized environment is commendable," she says. Added Kennedy, bragging of the state's leadership with an unintentionally hilarious reference to

Massachusetts's heinous car insurance system: "If you look at [mandatory] auto insurance, the first state to have it was Massachusetts. It set the example for the nation," and would now do the same for health care.

Yet in some cases, the self-congratulatory testimony of local boomer pols unwittingly serves as a damning confession that this latest Massachusetts Miracle is more feel-good mirage than substance. "We tell people not to look at our law as a policy blueprint," says former Democratic legislator John McDonough, head of a local health-care-reform lobbying group. "It's a political blueprint. You can take the dynamic and the ideas to trigger a new and more ambitious conversation in your state." Or you could be honest about the discouraging truth of the bill's passage, as Fehrnstrom was in an unguarded moment during our interview. "It probably wouldn't have happened if we didn't have the sword of [$770 million in] lost federal funds hanging over the State House," he admits. "Those types of achievement are too rare. And there was a period of time when we were trying to give birth to health-care reform when we bit our tongue on a lot, because we knew if they felt personal antagonism toward the governor they would walk away from reform, federal funds notwithstanding."

Liberal Democratic lawmakers willing to blow off desperately needed funds for the disabled and elderly out of mere personal spite for another politician? When it's not happening as a result of the apparently unbridgeable partisan, social, and cultural gap between Romney and Beacon Hill Democrats, it's Massachusetts Democrats who are falling on each other like jackals. "That's why the House and the Senate are so often at loggerheads," observes Fehrnstrom. "Personal slights become magnified in the minds of the leadership and their respective staffs. And they use their policymaking power to get even."

If this ugly equation of altruism and the public interest with narcissistic posturing and personal score settling sounds familiar, perhaps it's because we've seen boomer congressional and presidential leadership from Bill Clinton and Newt Gingrich to Dennis Hastert and George W. Bush draw the same self-serving connections as they've made a hash of assorted foreign and domestic policies. Mitt Romney regales conservative audiences on the campaign trail with jokes about fighting the lonely fight in Massachusetts as "a cattle rancher at a vegetarian convention." But Romney and his party don't have halos waiting for them at the hatcheck. By abandoning his moderate rhetoric on abortion and gay rights in a rush to the right as he fed his Potomac fever from 2004 on, Romney gave his Democratic enemies the tools they needed to dismember his approval rating and win back the governor's office in 2006. As he prepared to leave office, his competitors on the right threw his equivocations back in his face. A recycled 1994 Romney statement that he was trying to move on from the "Reagan-Bush" era won him a sharp rebuke from a South Carolina activist who backed John McCain in 2000, warning Romney that "you cannot slam Ronald Reagan or disrespect Ronald Reagan in a state like South Carolina." A fully engaged Romney, downplaying social positions that few Massachusetts voters support and using the threat of a second term to enhance his clout, might have gotten more done for the beleaguered working classes here. Instead, Romney leaves behind a compelling diagnosis of what's wrong with Kennedy country, but no antidote.

"I'm afraid my liberal friends too often are not willing to recognize the second-order effect of their policies, but instead seize the politics," he says. "They have, out of an abundance of compassion, promoted policies that have led to a personal underclass. Giving the poor money and housing vouchers and medical vouchers and food stamps seems compassionate, but unless you're very careful you actually encourage poverty and lock people into a culture of poverty. It's the same thing with the minimum wage; boosting it sky high is politically popular, but what's the second-order effect?"

Massachusetts voters put Romney into office out of despair over a moribund economy and a stagnant political culture unwilling or unable to craft workable solutions. That same culture gratuitously shunned Romney and his ideas because it couldn't distinguish between its personal instincts and the public interest, a distinction Romney himself has struggled with as his White House dreams evolved. The sad story of the Romney years in Massachusetts, then, begs his own question about the "second-order effect" theory that both boomer liberals and conservatives need to answer: "Do they really know those effects, but they're so attracted to the rhetoric and the political game that they ignore them?"

CHAPTER NINE

....

"What the F___ Is a Holiday Tree?"

THE PRESS RELEASE from a local public relations firm announcing the annual delivery of Boston's official Christmas tree in mid-November 2005 almost got overlooked when it came into the WBZ-TV newsroom. It was the thirty-fourth consecutive year that the people of Nova Scotia had donated a huge white spruce to Boston, a traditional show of thanks for the city's fast response to a catastrophic 1917 explosion in Halifax Harbor that killed hundreds. Normally, the arrival of the tree by truck was little more than a voice-over at the end of the newscast, a "sign of the season" kicker that served as a cue for anchor banter about early Christmas shopping. But this year's release came with a curious attachment: a statement from the City of Boston's Parks and Recreation Department welcoming the arrival of "Boston's Official Holiday Tree" and touting the forthcoming "Official Holiday Tree Lighting."

"What the f___ is a holiday tree?" growled my producer, Casey Sherman, as he threw the press releases on my desk with the disdain of a dog walker discarding an especially messy batch of droppings. Down on Boston Common, interviewing passersby as workers erected the tree, the mix of anger and disgust in his question was evident in both younger and older onlookers. "It's a Christmas tree; it's Christmas season," said one thirty-five-year-old tourist. "It's not a holiday tree; it's a Christmas tree," insisted a nineteen-year-old black man in a do-rag. "It's supposed to gather families together and bring in Christmas." Added an elderly city worker watching the tree go up from the cab of his truck, "I never heard of a Thanksgiving tree. I never heard of a Chanukah tree. This is for Christmas." Only one boomer woman, immaculately turned out and pushing her toddler in a high-priced stroller, seemed to embrace the politically correct terminology. "My first reaction was, it's a holiday tree," she said. "It's the holiday season—Thanksgiving and Christmas and Kwanzaa and Chanukah and New Year's. That denotes the holiday season for me."

That night on the air, we played the story for sarcastic laughs; I pointed out that it would be just a matter of days now before we all gathered with friends and family around the "traditional Thanksgiving bush"; the anchorman wished me a Happy Festivus, the ersatz "holiday for the rest of us" popularized on *Seinfeld*. But in Massachusetts and across the country, a popular culture saturated with gratuitous political correctness wasn't in a laughing mood. Boston mayor Tom Menino was furious with his own Parks Department, declaring, "I grew up with a Christmas tree; I'm going to stay with a Christmas tree." Televangelist Jerry Falwell weighed in on national TV, threatening a lawsuit and decrying "a concerted effort to steal Christmas." The student editor of a Christian journal at Harvard argued that "we should be celebrating our religious diversity instead of covering it up with bland inanities about 'holiday trees.'" And Donnie Hatt, the Nova Scotia logger who cut down the tree, said he would have "put it through the chipper" if he'd known it would be given a politically correct name: "If they decide it should be a holiday tree, I'll tell them to send it back. If it was a holiday tree, you might as well put it up at Easter."

To Tom Frank in *What's the Matter with Kansas?* the uproar over Boston's "holiday tree" seems to fit the mold of a prime weapon of mass manipulation from the conservative culture-war arsenal, the "plen-T-plaint . . . a curious amassing of petty, unrelated beefs with the world . . . the modus operandi for that cyberspace favorite, the political-correctness scoreboard, in which ridiculous examples of liberal intolerance (hypersensitive minorities, discrimination against Christmas, silly mascot issues) are heaped up by the thousands." Frank ridicules the plen-T-plaint for its implication that "liberalism can be held responsible for the world around us. . . . It doesn't matter that liberals have long since lost their power over government." In Kansas, perhaps. But not in Massachusetts, where political correctness is the signature cultural statement of the ruling elites, undermining their moral authority and driving a wedge between them and the working classes far more effectively than any right-wing demagogue could hope for.

The "holiday tree" affair wasn't the only eruption of political correctness to mar the 2005 holiday season here. At the Lowell Elementary School in Watertown, a liberal Boston suburb, a traditional December crafts bazaar was scrubbed by school administrators because a small percent of the items for sale were religious in nature. Meanwhile, an in-class show-and-tell Ramadan party at the same school was allowed to go forward. In Medway, an affluent commuter town southwest of the city, a sixth-grade teacher sent home red and green elf hats sewn by a parent because the colors represented Christmas, and students in the school choir were forced to drop "We Wish You a Merry Christmas" from their program and substitute the words "swinging holiday" for "Merry Christmas" in a song that made the cut. "I don't care if my child sings a Jewish song or a Kwanzaa song," said Medway School Committee member Kelly O'Rourke. "But where's my Christmas song?"

As usual, it's unclear which came first, actual complaints from parents or children about the religious oppressiveness of red and green elf hats, or the supposition that—this being Massachusetts—such complaints would be sure to follow. "All it takes is one person to be offended and our school will ban it," says Andrea Newman of the Underwood Elementary School her two sons attend in Newton, a city west of Boston that is so liberal that one school insists on calling a tug-of-war the "tug-of-peace." Sure enough, Underwood principal David Castelline canceled the school's fourteen-year-old tradition of teachers donning costumes and leading the children in Halloween arts-and-crafts projects. "I felt the goal was really important to make it a respectful and open and welcoming place for all members of our community," said Castelline, explaining his decision to replace the Halloween event with a "celebration of fall."

But Andrea Newman, noting the diversity of the racially mixed multilingual school population, wonders if political correctness might lead to a less welcoming environment. "What's next?" she says. "If they can cancel Halloween, what about Valentine's Day?" Good call. At the Bennett-Hemenway School in Natick, another western suburb, Valentine's Day is permitted, but in politically correct, gender-blind form. Says the principal, "If you are going to send a card to one girl or boy in the class, you have to send one to every boy and girl." And if children are to be shielded from the potential self-esteem damage of Valentine giving, who's to say government shouldn't step in to protect adults from the pernicious influence of that trans-fat gobbling, swinish reindeer oppressor who starts showing up each year soon after the holiday tree arrives? In Cambridge City Hall, a fellow employee who picks your name from a hat and anonymously gives you a small gift is called your "Secret Friend," a city spokesman explains, "in honor of all the holidays the occur at this time of year."

Perhaps it's just as well that Massachusetts schoolkids get exposed to political correctness at a young age, the better to prepare them for the onslaught awaiting them on Massachusetts college campuses. A 2005 incident at Harvard University involving Jada Pinkett-Smith, wife of Hollywood megastar Will Smith, underscored the thorough triumph of identity politics over common sense within boomer culture. Pinkett-Smith was the latest in a string of celebrities honored by the Harvard

Foundation for Intercultural and Race Relations as a way to spur fund-raising. She hosted the foundation's twentieth annual Cultural Rhythms show, featuring the Kuumba Singers, the Harvard Ballet Folklórico de Aztlán, and the Harvard Philippine Forum, which fused hip-hop with a traditional ethnic dance involving long bamboo rods, to the delight of Hakeem Rahim, a 2002 Harvard graduate with seemingly little time to follow world news: "The influence of hip hop really shows how much the global community is coming together."

Then Pinkett-Smith addressed the students, describing how she overcame her birth to teenage heroin addicts to realize her dreams. "Don't let anybody define who you are," she said. "Don't let them put you in a box. Don't be afraid to break whatever ceiling anybody has put on you. Women, you can have it all—a loving man, devoted husband, loving children, a fabulous career. They say you gotta choose. Nah, nah, nah. We are a new generation of women. We got to set a new standard of rules around here. You can do whatever it is you want. All you have to do is want it."

Dr. S. Allen Counter, director of the Harvard Foundation, was thrilled with her presentation, calling it "the best we've had thus far. Usually, the celebrities give warm thanks, but she sat down and talked to us. She was like a visiting professor, giving a perspective students don't always get to hear around here."

Days later, Counter and the foundation found themselves apologizing for Pinkett-Smith's comments, and pledging to "take responsibility to inform future speakers that they will be speaking to an audience diverse in race, ethnicity, religion, sexuality, gender and class." What went wrong? According to an on-campus group, the Bisexual, Gay, Lesbian, Transgender, and Supporters Alliance (BGLTSA), Pinkett-Smith's ode to her successful marriage was "extremely heteronormative, and made BGLTSA members feel uncomfortable," said group cochair Jordan Woods. "Our position is that the comments weren't homophobic, but the content was specific to male-female relationships." Added Margaret Barusch, Woods's cochair: "The comments had a very strong focus for an extended period of time on how to effectively be in a relationship—a heterosexual relationship. I don't think she meant to be offensive but I just don't think she was that thoughtful." And to Harvard Foundation member Yannis Paulus, Pinkett-Smith's crime was to tell the story of her life without manipulating those very personal details to somehow include every conceivable acronym within the student audience. "She wasn't trying to be offensive," he said. "But some felt she was taking a narrow view, and some people felt left out."

In the realm of Massachusetts boomer liberalism, the hurt feelings of "exclusion" of a bisexual, gay, lesbian, or transgendered listener from a talk given by a heterosexual is a serious problem to be weighed and discussed, with steps taken to prevent any reoccurrence. Of significantly less concern are the hopes of local workers for future employment that may have been stunted by the 2006 liberal jihad that drove Larry Summers from the Harvard presidency. Summers, a key player in life-science research initiatives that are a vital part of the state's economic future, lacked diplomatic and personal skills. But no one disputes that he was driven from office by left-wing faculty livid over his politically incorrect statements about patriotism, the right of Israel to exist, and the possible reasons behind a lack of female representation in the sciences. Immediate cost to the university: a $100 million grant from Oracle founder Larry Ellison to find solutions to problems in government health-care programs, withdrawn after the Summers resignation. Tom Finneran, the former House Speaker turned head of the Massachusetts Biotechnology Council, told me he heard from several overseas investors in the immediate wake of Summers's resignation expressing concern over whether a state that would countenance the removal of a key civic leader over such trivia was a stable place for investment.

No one need worry about Harvard's financial future. But the University of Massachusetts is a different story. The flagship campus at Amherst, like the rest of the twenty-nine-campus state higher-education system, struggles to provide decent instruction and facilities for more than 25,000 students. Many classes are overcrowded; much of the infrastructure is ancient and crumbling. No wonder. Massachusetts ranks 47th in the nation in state spending on public higher education per capita, 49th out of the fifty states in spending on higher education per $1,000 of state income (only Alabama is stingier). It is the only state in America spending less on public higher ed than it was a decade ago. Since all new job growth here over the past two decades has been in professions that require a college degree, it's no surprise that the locals, long since priced out of the prestigious private colleges, have flocked to state schools. But as enrollments soared by 5 percent over the first half of this decade, funding was cut by 25 percent on Beacon Hill, and student aid dropped by 13 percent. James Hayes-Bohanan, an associate geography professor, observes, "Massachusetts is the only state I have lived in where public higher education is considered somehow inferior. In most states, many political and business leaders are graduates of state colleges and universities. It is only in Massachusetts that such leaders come mainly from private schools, and therefore perpetuate an inferiority complex among those associated with state colleges."

If ever there was a place that needed to squeeze every nickel to prepare its students for white-collar job opportunities that may not hang around if a skilled workforce isn't cultivated, it's UMass Amherst. But university officials seem determined to lead the nation in a category of little evident usefulness to its working-class clientele. A mix of boomer academics who work at one of the five colleges in the area and liberals drawn to Amherst's bohemian setting (in the heart of the Pioneer Valley, sarcastically referred to by some as "happy valley") have long since turned the place into a nationally recognized citadel of political correctness. Once the home of deep thinkers like Emily Dickinson and Robert Frost, Amherst is now the scene of a never-ending string of PC psychodramas, like the debate over whether building a garage for town vehicles would constitute inappropriate endorsement of the internal combustion engine. Or like the rejection of a state-funded survey of teen substance abuse because the results might lead to racial profiling. Amherst often gets hot and bothered over issues of national identity. In 2001, some residents complained that the town was flying its newly acquired batch of American flags too often. A debate on the issue at a town meeting yielded a compromise agreement to limit their display to patriotic holidays, but not before UMass physics professor Jennie Traschen denounced Old Glory as "a symbol of terrorism and death and fear and destruction and repression." (A subsequent, lightly attended rally at Amherst College in support of the flag ended badly when "self-styled anarchists" took the stage and set two flags ablaze.) Coming on the eve of the terrorist attacks on New York and Washington, the Traschen comments drew international attention and angry national ridicule.

But in a town with just a 5 percent African American population, it's race that really triggers the politically correct instincts of Amherst's white liberals. Most famously, an attempt at Amherst Regional High School to stage *West Side Story*, the iconic Stephen Sondheim/Leonard Bernstein musical about interracial romance blossoming amid ethnic and racial tensions, ran afoul of student and parent protests. "It's a very racist play . . . replete with racial discrimination creating negative images of Puerto Ricans," complained one parent. The musical is "deeply problematic," declared UMass/Amherst poetry professor Martin Espada, for its "stereotypes having to do with gangs, violence, hot temper, and especially machismo," caricatures that he claimed sprang from "Sondheim's white, liberal imagination." And what of the role of the heroine, Maria, whose story has been seen by generations of apparently troglodytic theatergoers as a triumph of love over racism? According to the local weekly newspaper, the *Valley Advocate,* Espada dismissed Maria as a symbol of "the Madonna side of the old Madonna-whore continuum," an analogy that evokes Rev. Jerry Falwell's memorable warning that the character

Tinky Winky from the popular children's TV show *Teletub-bies* was a proselytizing gay role model in sheep's clothing. "He is purple, the gay pride color," noted Falwell, "and his antenna is shaped like a triangle, the gay pride symbol."

You can imagine how the same Amherst crowd that nod-ded sympathetically at Espada's complaint howled over Fal-well's nonsense. In a politically correct environment such as this, certain topics become taboo, and racially tinged disputes about them that grown-ups ought to be able to handle can eas-ily mushroom into resource-sapping confrontations. During the 2004 UMass/Amherst student government elections, presi-dential candidate Patrick Higgins argued against a controver-sial plan to set aside seats on the student senate for members of ALANA, a coalition of "African, Latino/a, Asian/Pacific Is-lander, and Native American" students. In a continuation of friction that dates to a mid-1990s dustup between ALANA and white student senators over the minority students' hosting of a speech by Louis Farrakhan, ALANA accused Higgins of being a "racist." Higgins lost to the ALANA candidate. During a beer-fueled election night party, a Higgins supporter drew a caricature on the wall behind the candidate showing Higgins in full Ku Klux Klan costume clutching a burning cross, the words "Grand Wizard" across his chest. His tongue lolling from his mouth and a dazed, stupid look in his eyes, the comic-book Hig-gins was saying, "I love ALANA!"

Someone took pictures. The photos hit the Web. ALANA wanted Higgins out of student government, but UMass ad-ministrators went further, inflaming an all-out campus debate by claiming the incident rose to the level of racial "harassment," with one even referring to Higgins and his friends as "the KKK Nine." Their resignations didn't stop the PC frenzy. Alarmed by this latest evidence of endemic "racism" on campus, the university chancellor appointed a special Commission on Campus Diversity to review the situation.

They returned with some expensive recommendations. A cabinet-level office of "diversity and inclusion activities" was to be established, with full staffing and a budget ample enough to provide "incentives and rewards" for members of the UMass community who get with the program. There was fresh budgetary and staffing support for ALANA, with an enhanced role in "mentoring and advocacy" for minority students. There was a warning that recent rounds of budget cuts had damaged the university's existing "diversity and inclusion" programs. And there was this stern admonition: "The nation will be unable to maintain its global leadership in many disciplines and professions unless institutions of higher learning increase the successful recruitment, enrollment and graduation of women and individuals from racial and ethnic groups currently underrepresented in higher education. . . . Diversity and inclusion are so essential to the core mission of the Amherst campus that it must find or raise the financial resources necessary to support its efforts on matters related to diversity."

Boston attorney Harvey Silverglate, a civil libertarian who tracks politically correct offenses against the First Amendment, compared the UMass "KKK" cartoon case with the infamous 1988 lawsuit against *Hustler* by Jerry Falwell, which the Supreme Court threw out on the grounds that scathing parody using offensive symbols was protected free speech.

And he noted the sad irony of UMass paying lip service to minority needs while squandering the scarce dollars that could actually help address them. "In a system without the resources to support a full-time tenured faculty, at a campus that makes increasing use of part-time contract teachers but has become too expensive for most working-class and minority students to attend, the commission nonetheless concluded that another bureaucracy was needed to solve the 'problem' posed by an obvious parody," he wrote. "No wonder there's not enough money to fund poor kids' educations: what little piece of the pie was reserved for them is being spent on expensive thought reform."

Within boomer intellectual circles, the debate continues over whether political correctness is a necessary step toward creating a progressive social environment, or self-indulgent liberal foolishness, made to order for conservative exploitation. "When the media get locked in their Northeastern ghetto and become slaves of . . . fanatical special interests, the American audience ends up looking to conservative voices for common sense," argues Camille Paglia. "Political correctness . . . is a travesty of Sixties progressive values." Yet if all there was to political correctness were the minor incursions on culture and custom of pretentious, annoying, but ultimately marginal bores, bureaucrats, and petty tyrants, it might justify Tom Frank's dismissal of it all as "petty" grist for yet another contrived "plen-T-plaint."

But when political correctness tries to constrain our response to terror in the post-9/11 era, as Democrats in Congress found when their poll numbers plummeted amid hand-wringing over Bush-era counterterrorism measures, it verges on political suicide. In early 2006, Boston FBI agents traced a terror threat lodged against Brandeis University, a nearby Jewish college, back to a public computer at the main library in Newton. They rushed to the library to search for leads, but the librarian refused to allow them to search the computers until they obtained a warrant, nearly nine hours later. Local liberals applauded. National reaction was typified by a poster to a Boston newspaper chat room: "First, they came into a public place, not a private home. Second, what are law-abiding people really worried about—that President Bush is going to find out how many Danielle Steel books you've checked out? And third, what good are civil liberties if you're pushing up daisies?"

Political embarrassment aside, when a show of force by petulant Harvard PC police gives pause to potential investors in Massachusetts's economic future, and when precious public-education resources are squandered on politics at a time of desperate need among blue-collar students, political correctness in its full Massachusetts flowering becomes significantly more toxic than just a bad joke. And for citizens stuck in crime-riddled urban neighborhoods where organized, violent gangs of kids as young as ten have been spotted, the PC instinct that thrives here is potentially life-threatening.

In late 2006, movie audiences across the country lapped up Martin Scorsese's take on the legend of Whitey Bulger, *The Departed*. The film evokes well-deserved contempt for the corrupt federal agents who covered for Bulger's prodigious drug dealing and serial killing. But so far, no one's made a movie about the politically correct attitudes, still thriving in the bluest state, that enabled Massachusetts's most famous living murderer after Bulger and helped cost the Democrats the presidency.

In 1974, Willie Horton and two accomplices, not content with merely robbing a seventeen-year-old gas station attendant in Lawrence, a poor immigrant city near the New Hampshire border, stabbed him nineteen times and left him to bleed to death. Horton took the fall for murder and got life. But in Massachusetts, his crime didn't disqualify him from taking unsupervised weekend furloughs. Failing to return from one furlough in 1986, Horton was in a Maryland prison a year later when he was convicted of raping a Maryland woman and knifing her fiancé when the man protested. The judge who sentenced him didn't hide his scorn for a Massachusetts request for extradition. "I'm not prepared to take the chance that Mr. Horton might again be furloughed or otherwise released," he said.

Amid national uproar over the furloughs, the brutalized Maryland couple traveled to Boston to plead with then governor Michael Dukakis for its repeal. But the governor refused to even meet with them. Dukakis, a self-described "card-carrying member of the ACLU," hadn't created the furlough rules, but he supported them. In his first term, he vetoed a bill that would have denied furloughs to first-degree murderers like Horton. And when the furloughs were raised as an issue in the 1988 Democratic primary campaign by Al Gore, Dukakis brushed off the question with typical hubris: "The difference between you and me is that I have run a criminal justice system. You haven't."

Dukakis went on to lose big to George H. W. Bush. Key contributing factors were Republican exploitation of the Horton case, which the Dukakis campaign ineffectually branded racist, and Dukakis's infamous failure in debate to express outrage at the notion of his own wife being raped and murdered, so eager was he to declare his opposition to capital punishment. A generation later, despite the political success story of Bill Clinton, a governor willing to execute a mentally retarded black man to demonstrate toughness on crime, in liberal Democratic circles the name Willie Horton remains synonymous with crude campaign race-baiting in particular and "unfair" smear tactics in general. (Thus, a 2004 Bush campaign ad painting John Kerry as soft on terrorism was branded "the Willie Horton ad of 2004" by a Kerry spokesman.) The furlough program that freed Horton to rape and pillage is long gone, but Massachusetts remains an easy mark for violent criminals, according to prosecutors and police in Manchester, New Hampshire, where a veteran cop was blown away in October 2006 by a twenty-six-year-old Bostonian with a long, violent rap sheet. Career thugs coming to New Hampshire from Massachusetts "seem to be getting lenient sentences thanks to lax practices south of the border," says Manchester police chief John Jaskolka. "When we go for a tougher sentence up here, (the courts) don't have the criminal background to do it."

Under Governor Deval Patrick, there seems little likelihood of dramatic change in that attitude. During the campaign, I surprised Patrick one day with questions about the Horton case:

Q: Would you have let Willie Horton out on furlough?

PATRICK: I have no idea about Willie Horton's background, history, what that furlough program is.

Q: Should first-degree murderers be eligible for furloughs?

PATRICK (tersely): Let me try to be clearer. The death penalty does not work. And in the case of those who are convicted of the most serious crimes, I believe in life without possibility of parole.

Q: Or furlough?

PATRICK (visibly angry): Without possibility of parole.

Later on in the race, when crime began to emerge as an issue, Patrick came out against furloughs for first-degree murderers. But he also backed restrictions on employer access to criminal records that were bitterly opposed by his two Democratic primary opponents, including the state's attorney general. And when Patrick's sympathy for rapist Benjamin LaGuer invited Republican attacks on his "softness" on crime that began cutting into his lead, Massachusetts liberals were quick to evoke their symbol of the venality of harsh criminal penalties. "Americans are so very stupid," commented a poster to the national left-wing blog Daily Kos. "The ghosts of '88 linger—Willie Horton is in the air." And the ultimate ghost of 1988, Dukakis himself, weighed in with his assessment of the "awful" campaign being waged against Patrick. "It makes Willie Horton look mild by comparison."

For Rev. Eugene Rivers, it was a familiar replay of the disengagement that political correctness promotes between liberal elites and the constituencies they purport to champion. "Even

Patrick, the black guy from the 'hood, can't engage in a rational conversation around here about the main issue that disproportionately affects the people who live in the circumstances he came from," says Rivers disgustedly. "It really is a question of intellectual bankruptcy."

CHAPTER TEN

....

The Big Pig
*(and the Fatal Consequences
of the Boomer Appetite for Pork)*

"THANK GOD, SHE didn't suffer," said Angel Del Valle, the forty-six-year-old Puerto Rican grocery-store clerk who never even heard his wife scream as she was crushed to death by the most expensive public-construction project in American history. "It was like a bomb."

The collapse of part of Boston's Big Dig onto Del Valle's car brought a horrific end to the American dream Angel and thirty-eight-year-old Milena Del Valle were living. They met in Jamaica Plain, a largely blue-collar Boston neighborhood with a large Hispanic population, where both were active at the Hispanic Community Church of Boston. She had a maintenance job at a restaurant and sometimes made extra money hawking copies of a Spanish weekly newspaper at local subway stations. He ran the meat counter at Hi-Lo Foods, a popular market with local Latinos. They lived in the standard housing of Boston's blue-collar workers, an apartment in a triple-decker. After work, friends said, he would do the cooking; after dinner, she would rub his tired feet.

Angel was returning the favor, massaging Milena's sore feet the night of July 10, 2006, when she insisted on changing out of her pajamas and going with him to Logan Airport to pick up his brother and sister-in-law. "Angel gets lost easy," a friend of Milena's said later. "She didn't want him out late by himself." So Milena accompanied her husband on the drive to Logan, a trip that had become much quicker since the opening three years before of the new tunnel under Boston Harbor linking downtown with the airport. There had been widespread praise for the improved access to Logan since then, a rare positive note for a landmark engineering project that had become an international symbol of political excess and incompetence even before it destroyed the Del Valle family.

Back in the mid-1980s, the Big Dig seemed like a no-brainer to fortysomething progressives like Gov. Michael Dukakis and his secretary of transportation, Fred Salvucci. An older generation of politicians had blighted downtown Boston with an elevated central artery that had quickly become the most congested strip of highway in America. The old Sumner and Callahan tunnels between the artery and the airport were perpetually in gridlock as well. The downtown business crowd implored Dukakis to build another tunnel; Salvucci's environmentalist pals wanted the artery gone and mass-transit expanded. The two men decided to try to please everyone. If

House Speaker Tip O'Neill of Cambridge could arrange for the grandiose artery-tunnel project to be classified as new interstate highway construction, the state could get uncapped federal funding of 90 percent of project costs. As John Farrell reports in his definitive biography *Tip O'Neill and the Democratic Century*, Federal Highway Administrator Ray Barnhart, a conservative Republican with little patience for what he called Massachusetts's "anti-transportation mode," was skeptical. "My first inclination was to let the bastards freeze in the dark," he said. "A real drum-beating yahoo," said Salvucci later of Barnhart. "He was out to croak us."

O'Neill had a good working relationship with President Ronald Reagan, but Reagan vetoed the Big Dig, calling it "a special interest project." Big Dig proponents decided they needed Republican help to override the veto. So among other moves, the state hired the GOP-connected engineering firm Bechtel to be construction manager. "I blew my stack," recalled Brian Donnelly, then a lunch-bucket Democratic congressman representing working-class neighborhoods of Boston. "Why not give the job to some guys from Dorchester? But that took care of the Republican opposition."

When the Big Dig finally got the green light in April 1987, its estimated cost was $3.1 billion. But according to Farrell, Tip was skeptical of the project's scale and management, and worried that what was already being called "Tip's Tunnel" would become known in time as "Tip's Folly." Said O'Neill, with the wisdom of experience, "The squeaky wheel gets the grease in Washington, there is no question about it. Maybe it's not the way to run a government, but that's the way the government runs."

Two decades later, as Angel and Milena Del Valle climbed into their fifteen-year-old Buick for the drive to the airport, the Big Dig had become the perfect storm of a political culture's arrogance and ineptitude, the boom generation's most grotesque character flaws coming together to create a Vietnam-like morass of fatally unchecked waste and incompetence.

The cost of the project was closing in on $15 billion, nearly five times the original estimate, as the state's boomer power brokers had proven incapable of responsible fiscal management. Everyone was feeding at the Big Dig trough, including the usual suspects: labor unions guaranteed inflated wages under politically motivated "project-labor" agreements; lawyers, accountants, and bankers harvesting windfalls from the huge bond transactions tied to the project's financing; and politicians at the local, state, and federal level, their palms greased by all of the above.

All that was business as usual. But the Big Dig was a coming-out party for a new boomer take on the time-honored practice of public-works-project feeding frenzy—the extortionate demands of "progressive" interests using the threat of legal action to shake down the taxpayers on a grand scale. In a 1994 review of the Big Dig's progress, with the price tag at a mere $7.7 billion, the *Boston Globe* found that the project's managers had made over a thousand "mitigation" commitments totaling $2.8 billion, more than a third of the total cost. "Neighborhood groups, environmentalists, developers, parking-lot owners, politicians, gadflies—all of them sought what they could get . . . when they realized that the state could be pressured into paying for their favorite causes if they would drop their opposition to the mammoth project," the *Globe* reported. Most of the "mitigation" spending actually had little to do with the direct impact of the Big Dig. It was pork, pure and simple, extracted by politicians and activists intent on, as Salvucci himself once described it, "delivering some chunk of mastodon meat back to the tribe." And even the most altruistic petitioners didn't much care about the cost to the taxpayers. The architect of the largest single payoff, Doug Foy of the nonprofit Conservation Law Foundation, won a state commitment to a series of public transit improvements with a projected cost of $3.6 billion, but admitted later that the price tag "was not something that we thought was our responsibility." (Years later as a member of Romney's cabinet overseeing public transit investments, Foy was critical of the deal's costs, arguing they were simply unaffordable.)

Another boomer trait paving the Big Dig's catastrophic path was unwarranted hubris, the belief among its builders and planners that they could make dubious or untried techniques work where others could not. One of the project's key political patrons, former Massachusetts governor William Weld, liked to boastfully compare the project with the Great Pyramid of Giza, one of the original Seven Wonders of the World. "The Central Artery project has enough engineering marvels to fill a textbook," gushed the project Web site, touting the Big Dig's unprecedented use of slurry-wall construction in its tunnels as "the single most important construction technique on this gigantic project." But gushing of a different sort made fools of the Big Dig's builders in 2004, when a huge breach in the tunnel sent water pouring onto the roadway.

Investigators found that contractors had failed to thoroughly remove debris from the vaunted slurry walls, so that when concrete was poured, weak pockets were formed that later caved to
water pressure. The project, they discovered, was riddled with
such leaks.

The video of water cascading into the tunnel, like a scene
from *The Poseidon Adventure*, touched off a round of typically
Bostonian black humor about a new use for the swan boats and
the world's most expensive car wash. But it also provided
graphic new evidence of a truth that the boomer political establishment had worked hard to suppress—the self-congratulatory
builders of "the greatest engineering project in the history of the
world" often didn't know what the hell they were doing. As
early as 1994, top project managers admitted to reporters that
the complex project was replete with engineering mistakes and
planning miscalculations. A new engineer coming on the job
in 1997 found that design drawings done by Bechtel had completely omitted the presence, hard by the heart of the Central
Artery tunnel construction, of the Fleet Center, Boston's
19,600-seat home to the hockey Bruins and basketball Celtics.
The massive arena "fell through the cracks," a Bechtel supervi-
sor acknowledged. Cost to the taxpayers of this gaffe: $991,000.
But a *Globe* investigation found that Bechtel and its contractors
never paid back a dime in compensation, nor were they asked to
by any state or federal officials.

In fact, far more energy had been spent on covering up
problems and quieting critics of the Big Dig than on taking
any steps to improve on a nearly two-decade track record of
costly neglect and error on the part of the designers and con-

tractors and their purported public-sector overseers. In 1994, Democratic gubernatorial nominee Mark Roosevelt tried to make incumbent governor Weld's mismanagement of the project a campaign issue; his charges were largely ignored, and he was buried on Election Day. The same fate befell Republican state treasurer Joe Malone, who made the Big Dig a centerpiece of his GOP primary challenge to Weld's successor, Paul Cellucci. "The pressure from the business community and from the editorial pages was intense," recalls Eric Fehrnstrom, Romney's aide, who back then served in a similar role for Malone. Publicly and privately, says Fehrnstrom, a bipartisan array of the biggest figures in the Massachusetts political establishment delivered the same message: "don't politicize this issue; this is a project that is good for the region; for the benefit of everybody you should just be quiet."

But the cover-up began to come apart in late 1999, with the discovery that Big Dig officials had, as a federal audit put it, "repeatedly and deliberately" failed to disclose massive cost overruns on the project in "one of the most flagrant breaches of the integrity of the federal-state partnership in the history of the nearly 85-year-old federal-aid highway program."

Massachusetts boomers had inherited from their elders a mandate to think big and bulldoze obstacles. The Big Dig, after all, was the last major unfinished link in the federal highway system that was the prior generation's proudest domestic achievement, a precursor to JFK's pledge to go to the moon. "Now gaining real power, Boomers do not inherently dislike government," despite their early protest experiences, write

William Strauss and Neil Howe in *Generations*. "Their task is to redirect public institutions toward what they consider a socially redemptive purpose, casting aside [their parents'] preoccupation with process and expertise." The Big Dig was about to be exposed as a case study in the grievous risk posed to the public's finances, confidence in government, and physical well-being when boomers with power convince themselves that their excesses, blunders, and self-serving rationalizations of it all constitute progress marching on.

In May 2000, Arizona senator John McCain held a hearing on the mess before his Senate Committee on Commerce, Science and Transportation that left him visibly appalled. After listening to project bigwigs proclaim their pride in a project that "has met or exceeded all of its professional obligations," McCain zeroed in on the details. He challenged Andrew Natsios, the newly appointed "reformer" sent in by Gov. Paul Cellucci to clean up the mess, to explain his approval of a $200,000 severance—a year's pay—given to the former Big Dig chairman held responsible for the cost-overrun cover-up.

"One year is fairly standard in state government," explained Natsios. "He asked for three years. We gave him one year. That's Turnpike money, not federal money. I acted in what I thought was the public's interest."

McCain's eyebrows arched. "You have an interesting way of looking at things, Mr. Natsios," he said.

McCain challenged the "cost-plus" contractual arrangement worked out between the state and Bechtel, which virtually gave the contractors a blank check to fill out at a later date. "It's not an abnormal method of contracting," said Matthew

Wiley of Bechtel. "It's how they do it for major projects all around the world."

McCain pounced. "I would allege that in places all over the world, there would be some financial penalty to be paid. You sign contracts based on assumptions and when those assumptions are wrong and it costs more taxpayer dollars, somebody should be held responsible rather than just proceeding on. If that's satisfactory to you, business as usual, that's fine, but there should be some penalty associated with people not being able to fulfill their contractual obligations. I don't know many places in the world that would submit or accept this kind of performance."

And McCain's most vivid moment of apoplexy came after he read into the record a hostile letter to federal auditors from Big Dig project director Patrick Moynihan challenging their preliminary estimate that the project was $942 million over budget. Just three months after that forecast, project officials were forced to admit the true cost overrun was more than $1.4 billion. But in full cover-up mode, Moynihan had charged that the feds had "foisted on the public" a cascade of "factual errors, misstatements, and misleading calculations" that betrayed "a fundamental lack of understanding of how a multibillion-dollar megaproject needs to be managed."

"When the people in charge write this response," snapped McCain, waving a copy of Moynihan's letter, "that's a remarkable situation. It's something, in all candor, I haven't experienced before. There's no factual basis. That kind of thing deteriorates the role of the oversight of the government. This is really a bit disconcerting as to how those individuals who commanded this project view the role of the government and the administration of American taxpayer dollars."

Incredibly, the worst was yet to come. But the unraveling of the Big Dig's mismanagement was at least a wake-up call for Christy Mihos, a mild-mannered convenience store magnate from Boston's South Shore who had been appointed to the Massachusetts Turnpike Authority board of directors in 1998. A veteran party donor and activist, Mihos was a typical boom-era Massachusetts Republican, liberal on social issues such as abortion rights and gay marriage, moderate on economic matters, and most energized by the notion of governmental waste.

The revelations of hidden cost-overruns embarrassed Mihos and fellow board member Jordan Levy, a Democrat, who had been signing off unquestioningly on Big Dig contracts. The two men began demanding more information about the design changes that were escalating costs. Over management objections, they voted to hire an outside engineer to review Bechtel's work, and contested huge toll hikes proposed to subsidize the project. Alarmed Bechtel officials met with the new governor, Republican Jane Swift, who took steps to remove them from the board.

Mihos had the ear of reporters covering the Big Dig, who found his concerns about the mishandling of project details almost unfailingly on target. He also had the attention of federal investigators, who relied on him as a key source for their probes of Big Dig malfeasance. But in the editorial boardrooms and across the boomer establishment, despite all that had transpired, the wagons were circled. A *Globe* editorial trashed Mihos and Levy as "fiscally irresponsible" and "reckless," insisting, in a by-now familiar refrain, that their presence on the board "threatens the completion of the Central Artery project." Swift's firing of the two dissidents—a move later reversed by the state supreme court—was endorsed by an array of prominent business groups, including the Greater Boston Chamber of Commerce. In one especially memorable episode played out in front of local TV news cameras, a top Big Dig lawyer berated Mihos for allegedly undermining the project's credibility by saying in a 2002 cable TV interview: "The politicians try and move this thing forward so quickly that the contracts go out, and they're not totally designed. Unless someone is diligent and stringent about watching these cost overruns, that's where everything just gets unglued."

Talk about prescience. In September 2004, the tunnel wall breached, stalling traffic and sparking an investigation that founds hundreds of leaks and widespread shoddy workmanship. In May 2006, six managers at a project subcontractor were indicted for delivering 5,000 truckloads of tainted concrete to Big Dig worksites, a case that is still pending. But none of that dampened the celebration on June 5, 2006, when the Central Artery tunnel was dedicated to the memory of Tip O'Neill. Christy Mihos, his term on the board unrenewed by Gov. Mitt Romney, did not attend. But Mike Dukakis was there, wedged between John Kerry and Ted Kennedy. Paul Cellucci and his old Big Dig partner, Jim Kerasiotes, were in attendance, along with Jane Swift and an array of the lobbyists, union leaders, and lawyers who made small fortunes off the project. And they all applauded warmly when Kerry validated their $14.6 billion baby. "Within a few years, those who were sometimes critical of this project, those who worried about its cost, are going to look back and they're not going to see the cost," said Kerry. "The fact is, this tunnel will be a bargain and, more importantly, it will be one of this country's greatest public projects in history."

Thirty-five days later, about a mile from the scene of this festival of boomer backslapping, a bolt holding a three-ton concrete slab to the roof of the I-90 connector tunnel gave way above Milena Del Valle. Investigators focused on improperly prepared epoxy used to secure the bolt. The Big Dig, just as Christy Mihos had predicted, had become unglued.

Public reaction was intense. "For decades we have collectively turned our heads or become resigned to a corrupt network of unions, politicians, government agencies, and businesses that conspire to gain the maximum financial and political advantage at the lowest cost to themselves," wrote Martin Ross of Rockport in a blistering letter to the *Globe*. "Feeding at the public trough has been institutionalized here far more than anywhere else I have lived in this country." Former attorney general Scott Harshbarger, who had futilely challenged Cellucci's management of the Big Dig as the Democratic nominee for governor in 1998, called the project "the equivalent of Enron and WorldCom . . . a conspiracy of all sectors and leaders of silence, cheerleading, spin, and no concern for oversight, transparency, disclosure or accountability."

But it was left to Christy Mihos—who coincidentally, when the tunnel collapsed, was in the middle of a long-shot independent run for governor—to connect the Big Dig fiasco with the broader plight of working-class residents, still alive unlike the luckless Milena Del Valle, but barely hanging on. In a speech to the same Greater Boston Chamber of Commerce that had supported his firing for whistle-blowing five years earlier, Mihos was blunt. "I was right about the Big Dig," he said to a smattering of applause. But the megadisaster was just a symbol of a political culture's failure, which had brought the state "to her knees," he continued. "There are many people in this room who represent the special interests and do very, very, very well. But you go down to Cape Cod where I live right now; there are 3,400 homes for sale down there because the elderly and people on fixed incomes and people who don't make the big bucks and can't afford property taxes are being forced out of their homes. This state . . . is eminently unaffordable."

Just as in the halcyon days before the Big Dig slaughtered its first customer, there was interest in—but little real market for— Mihos's message. He drew less than 10 percent of the vote in the November election, his message of change thoroughly co-opted by Deval Patrick. And in a final boomer flourish to the sorry Big Dig saga, it appears the orgy of public hand-wringing about the need for reform in the way Massachusetts does business hasn't yet resulted in enhanced listening skills. Within days of the fatal ceiling collapse, several local companies specializing in structural analysis technology had reached out to the state to help with inspection work on the Big Dig tunnels, now believed to be riddled with safety issues. None of them got a response. State engineers rely, according to a state official, on "visual inspections that are fairly rudimentary"—e.g., flashlights and eyeballs. Says the appalled head of one local company that uses ultrasound to evaluate tunnel safety, "We'll probably find out who killed Kennedy before we find out what happened in there." But we needn't wait to draw conclusions about the boomer character flaw exposed by the whole fiasco. All of the boom generation's homage to healthier lifestyles may be borne out in their eating habits. But the relentless lip service to reform and modernity among Massachusetts's boomer politicians falls flat when confronted with the fatal, costly consequences of their compulsive bingeing on pork.

CHAPTER ELEVEN

....

In Your Backyard, Not Mine

AS TEENAGERS GROWING up in Cambridge, when there was nothing doing in Harvard Square and we were getting hungry, we would often bike over to a friend's house with an amply stocked fridge. The house was about a mile away, down one of America's most elegant avenues. Leafy Brattle Street draws crowds to gawk at its elegant mansions, which once belonged to loyalists to the British crown. The historic neighborhood includes the residence of nineteenth-century poet Henry Wadsworth Longfellow and, in more recent times, former governor William Weld and scores of other ultrarich luminaries. It's a beautiful stretch of ultraexpensive real estate, and one summer Saturday in the early 1970s, a friend and I were taking our time pedaling to our buddy's place for the usual pantry raid. The first time the Cambridge police cruiser passed us, I hardly noticed. The second time, I figured they were making rounds. On the third pass they pulled us over and asked our names, where we were from, who we were going to visit. They looked us up and down, told us to be careful, and went on their way.

"What was that about?" I said to my friend as we pedaled away.

"What do you think?" he spat back.

Two kids on bikes, one white, one black. Someone on Brattle Street had dropped a dime.

Nearly twenty years later, nothing much had changed along Brattle Street, the ultimate address of privilege in a city that fancies itself the most broad-minded place in America. Brattle Street neighbors of the Commonwealth Day School, a small private kindergarten catering to black students, were in front of the Cambridge Zoning Board of Appeals, trying to stop the school from offering classes through grade seven. The Brattle Street Victorian in question, right next door to Longfellow House, had been home to a prep school for decades, where the students sometimes raced cars, littered, and double-parked. When the Commonwealth Day School bought the property, there was no red carpet unrolled. The neighbors got a temporary cease-and-desist order, then fought the school's occupancy permit. At the zoning board meeting, their lawyer presented 235 signatures on a petition opposing the special permit the school needed to expand. Among the signers: local liberal icons such as Harvard Law School professor Laurence Tribe, cofounder of the American Constitution Society, whose mission includes promoting "means of combating inequality resulting from race, color, [and] ethnicity."

The neighbors argued that the parcel wasn't zoned for institutional use, despite its long history of just such use, and that the school would generate unbearable traffic and parking problems. The zoning board voted unanimously to grant the school its permit, but attached strict requirements for off-street student drop-off, staggered arrival times, and a traffic monitor. None of it mollified the residents, some of them veterans of a successful battle to keep the John F. Kennedy Presidential Library and Museum from being built on an old MBTA yard a mile away. "I guess the city thinks Brattle Street has a higher tolerance than other areas," sniffed one abutter. "I live with traffic and parking pressures most of the time," complained another. "I would say, right now, we are just about at the limit of our tolerance."

The Brattle Street residents denied that the race of their unwanted new neighbors was an issue, a claim school officials weren't buying. "It seems to me these people who live on Brattle Street are uncomfortable with black children . . . and are worried the value of their property will go down," said one long-time school board member. "If the school were all white, no one would have any problems." In the end, money talked and the Commonwealth Day School walked. The neighbors' legal battle dragged on to the point where their uncertain future forced the school to move back to Boston. Several years later, it closed for good. The Massachusetts attorney general brought suit against the neighbors and city officials, claiming that "these defendants apparently believe that personal wealth, influence and a fancy address entitle them to engage in racist behavior," but the case was later thrown out by a federal judge.

Prof. Tribe scrambled to escape a wave of caustic publicity generated by the Commonwealth Day School story, claiming he hadn't known what he was signing and offering to raise money for the school. "I am not in a position to impugn the motives of the group of neighbors involved and would not want to accuse them of racial prejudice . . . [but] I am suspicious, however, about why I was told so little about the facts when my name was solicited," Tribe said.

A decade later, the whole sorry story was still occasionally invoked in discussions of clandestine racism. "In Cambridge, people stay away from the kind of language that will get them labeled as racist," said one city councilor. "The buzzword these days is traffic. People don't say, 'we don't want that group here because of crime' anymore. They know better." And for Joan Wallace-Benjamin, the parent of a Commonwealth Day School student and president of the Urban League of Eastern Massachusetts, the whole episode was an unwanted lesson in the geographical limits of Brattle Street liberal tolerance. "My son has had a very interesting education in racial discrimination and prejudice at the tender age of 5," she said. "He was very much aware that much of the action that had been taken against the school was against the children and the color of their skin. There was no other way to paint it for the children and it wasn't painted any differently for the parents."

The old colonial-era nickname for Brattle Street—Tory Row, hung on Cambridge's royalists at a time when the label signaled unshakeable belief in the right of kings to dictate the future of the state—turns out to have embarrassingly enduring relevance. Massachusetts political and social elites profess a

profound belief in the notion of commonwealth, a governmental process committed to the common good. We are one of
only four states to retain that antique official designation: the
Commonwealth of Massachusetts. But again and again in the
era of liberal hegemony here, the power brokers get caught
drawing borders around how far the notion of commonwealth
really goes, boundaries that strikingly coincide with the plot
plan of their backyards.

The most notorious case study of liberal Massachusetts
NIMBYism (Not in My Backyard) was the court-ordered
Boston school desegregation of the mid-1970s. Vicious racists
in Boston city government had systematically denied black
schoolchildren equal access to a decent education for generations, flouting federal law in the process. A draconian remedy
was applied by federal district court judge Wendell Arthur
Garrity, a Kennedy family crony who took the commuter train
into the courthouse in Boston each day from his home in
Wellesley, a wealthy white suburb. Instead of easing desegregation into the racially polarized city through the early grades
or making well-heeled suburban school systems like Wellesley's part of the solution, Garrity immediately began busing
high-school students from Roxbury, the core of the black
ghetto, into high schools in Charlestown and South Boston, two
of the city's toughest white working-class neighborhoods. The
ensuing street violence—most notably, a Pulitzer prize–winning photo of a black man being clubbed with an American
flag by white thugs on City Hall Plaza—left a permanent stain
on the city's image. White and black parents with the resources
to do so fled the chaos. Private-school enrollment soared. Be-

tween 1970 and 1980, 12 percent of the city's population moved out, including one-third of the families with school-age children.

"Boston schools today are far more segregated than they were in 1974," notes Elliot Weinbaum in a 2004 analysis of Boston school desegregation for the University of Pennsylvania's Graduate School of Education journal. "The support that existed for the Garrity plan came from liberals in the suburbs who would be unaffected by it. The plan went largely unheeded by most Bostonians, black and white, who were tired of getting advice from people whose children would not be affected by any plan. Upon the start of busing, Mayor White commented: 'We've fought that suburban-siege mentality too long and too hard, and our efforts for metropolitan solutions have been resisted too consistently for us to trust that judgment or sincerity.'"

The fig leaf for Wellesley and other white, liberal suburbs was the Metropolitan Council for Educational Opportunity (METCO), a state-funded program that buses poor kids from the inner city to suburban school districts. Founded in the mid-1960s, METCO has always struggled to survive despite intense demand among families of color for relief from abysmal urban schools. Only a few dozen communities host the 3,300 METCO kids; the most recent waiting list had 15,500 names on it. But Wellesley's handful of urban refugees are just part of its story of racial healing; a few years back, the high-school football team, the Red Raiders, dropped the "Red" from its name out of concern for Native American sensitivities.

The small-bore signs of rampant NIMBYism keep piling

up. Ultraliberal Brookline, Michael Dukakis's hometown, where they famously balk at reciting the Pledge of Allegiance before town meetings, wanted to put up concrete barriers along part of its border with a dicey Boston neighborhood, but the story leaked out, and they retreated to a ban on overnight parking. Lincoln, a tony suburb near Wellesley, turned several arteries connecting it with blue-collar Waltham into one-way streets—outbound. A move to start regular freight and passenger ferry service to Martha's Vineyard and Nantucket from the impoverished immigrant city of New Bedford ran afoul of the likes of the Nantucket police chief, who complained that he didn't have a customs office to search New Bedford visitors for drugs. Said one island lawyer of his clients' conflict with New Bedford, "There's no real community of interest between the two."

In their protective blue-state cocoon, unchallenged by significant political or ideological opposition, Massachusetts liberal elites aren't often forced to find common interests, but are free to pander to the crowd and their own egos. Longtime alternative-energy champion John Kerry is quick to denounce the feds for failing to tighten fuel-efficiency standards that would render most gas-guzzling SUVs obsolete. Yet when I pointed out to Kerry that the Town and Country minivan he had pulled up in at a downtown Boston appearance averages less than 20 miles per gallon, he was unfazed. "I have a hybrid," he said, but offered no plans to dump the gas-guzzlers from his personal fleet. "I'm not gonna be a hypocrite about it. I'm gonna have a car that I enjoy driving still, and I'm gonna continue to do that. But I also am trying to make that effort [to drive fuel-efficient vehicles] where it works within the framework of what we're choosing to do. I encourage people to get them, but it's also fun to drive a fast car occasionally."

How special. It's also fun to sail the scenic waters of Nantucket Sound on a 60-foot ketch, as iconic former CBS anchorman Walter Cronkite used to do before advancing age grounded him. And when opponents of a 130-turbine wind farm, proposed for shallow shoals in the sound nearly nine miles off the coast of Martha's Vineyard, approached Cronkite about becoming a spokesman for their cause, he readily agreed. Cronkite didn't stop to think, he acknowledged later, about the plight of lower-income residents of the Cape and Islands in desperate need of the relief the so-called Cape Wind project could provide from ever-rising energy costs. Nor did he bother to fact-check the criticisms of its opponents, who draw some of their support from oil industry executives. "The most trusted man in America" had what he later termed a "hysterical" reaction to the thought of "such a ghastly invasion of this wonderful body of water." To his credit, Cronkite had second thoughts, and after meeting with Cape Wind officials, he dropped his major objections to the wind farm. He said he was impressed by the "sincerity and dedication of the principals," reassured to learn that seventeen different state and federal agencies were reviewing the plan, and convinced that the wind farm would be no threat to navigation. "It is a waste area, really," he said of the rocky Horseshoe Shoals site. "It's so shallow that it's almost like being on land. Nobody would sail through it."

That's far more credence than Ted Kennedy has ever placed on the facts about Cape Wind, which would be visible on the horizon from his family's legendary Hyannisport compound. Through the years, as the project passed exhaustive reviews by state and federal authorities and private environmental groups, Kennedy repeatedly tried to kill it, twice failing to have poison-pill language inserted through backroom legislative maneuvering. "Cape Wind hasn't met the test, and I doubt they ever will," he said at one point, even as the project continues to clear regulatory hurdles. His nephew, environmental lawyer Robert F. Kennedy Jr., was candid about his own motivation for opposing the project. "I think the first obligation of all environmentalists is to protect their own backyards," said Kennedy. "I don't live on the Cape, but I love that water body . . . and I don't want to see it devalued." As support for Cape Wind mushroomed among many of his traditional labor and environmental allies, and public support among beleaguered Massachusetts energy consumers approached landslide proportions, Ted Kennedy's position became palpably embarrassing for him. He shied away from questions about it in encounters with the local media. But when even the *Boston Globe* editorial page—traditionally a Kennedy ally—wrote that "the senator does expose himself to accusations of Not In My Back Yard–ism by opposing the project before environmental regulators have even begun to pass a verdict on it," Kennedy felt compelled to defend himself. "Far more is at stake in the decision than our backyards, and I make no apology for opposing this project now," he said in a written statement. Meanwhile, as Kennedy fumes and stalls, and his nephew Joe performs public relations stunts for Hugo Chavez to get energy relief to low-income Massachusetts residents, Texas is letting out the jib on a major wind farm in the Gulf of Mexico that could soon be producing cheap, clean power for 40,000 homes. There appear to be few political hurdles. "This is Texas," says state land commissioner Jerry Patterson. "We don't have Walter Cronkite and Ted Kennedy whining about their backyards."

Another classic NIMBY moment occurred a few years back when Shuttle America, a small regional airline running turboprop flights out of Hanscom Field in Boston's western suburbs, tried to expand its operations to include jets. Opponents from wealthy towns near the airfield, including Lexington and Concord, argued that their "fragile" historic landmarks would be threatened by more flights. "Jet traffic at Hanscom needs to be rolled back, not increased," declared Anna Winter of Save Our Heritage, a self-described historic preservation group. "If Shuttle America tries to bring jets here, it will face a storm of opposition that will make past protests look pale in comparison."

In the end, Shuttle America was chased away from Hanscom altogether, but not before Rev. John Hudson of the West Concord Union Church, quoting Gandhi's citation of "worship without sacrifice and politics without principle" as two of the seven deadly sins, put the protests in stark perspective. "The opposition here in Concord and other surrounding towns is about the phenomenon known as NIMBY," he wrote in a public letter. "Politicians feed off this self-centered civic frenzy. They pander to us citizens and we eat it up, buying into the myth that we can have it all, and not sacrifice anything."

Trying to match liberal boomer rhetoric with Me Generation lifestyles is tough sledding everywhere. But coming from a
liberal political culture that constantly extols its compassion for
the masses, the familiar Massachusetts sight of powerful elites
exempting themselves from the social "solutions" they so love
to impose on others is especially bracing.

There isn't a prominent Massachusetts political figure in
the past thirty years who hasn't emphatically called for more
affordable housing, not just subsidized apartments for the
poor, but decent starter homes and condos for the working
classes. Unfortunately, there's little to show for all that talk.
A 2003 survey found Massachusetts was the least affordable
state in the country for renters, and perennially among the top
three most expensive states in the nation to buy a house. The average single-family home costs well over $400,000, with prices
estimated to have risen by nearly 600 percent over the past
twenty-five years. Another study at the turn of the decade reported that someone earning the median state income could not
afford to buy a median-priced house in 118 of Greater Boston's
127 cities and towns.

Who suffers most from this chronic exclusivity? Researchers at UMass/Boston found that 55 percent of Latino
households and 42 percent of black households were among
the 27 percent of all households statewide that were "shelter
poor"—unable to meet minimum needs for food, clothing,
transportation and medical care because so much of their income goes to pay for housing. But regardless of fluctuations in
housing prices, availability keeps getting tighter. In the 1960s,
there were more than 172,000 new housing units permitted in

the Boston metro area; during the 1990s, only 84,000 permits were issued.

What gives? In a landmark study last year, Harvard economics professor Edward Glaeser conducted the most extensive survey yet of land use regulation by 187 cities and towns in central and eastern Massachusetts. He found a dizzying array of zoning and environmental rules had been constructed by boomer planners and politicians to make more housing development "difficult to impossible." Among the preferred NIMBY devices: huge minimum lot sizes that allow for McMansions but prevent affordable multiunit development; banning irregularly shaped lots; "growth caps" and "phasing schedules" that artificially restrict the number of new units that can be constructed in a given year; local wetland regulations that are tougher than the already strict state rules; septic-system regulations that often make new building prohibitively expensive; and a pantheon of construction-smothering subdivision rules, cluster provisions, and arcane zoning restrictions. If all else fails, call in the yellow spotted turtle, a species known to inhabit only twenty-four locations in Massachusetts two decades ago, when it was classified as a protected species. But life on the list of "species of special concern" has apparently been very, very good to the spotted turtle. Nearly a thousand separate turtle sightings at potential development sites in 2005 led to 281 environmental reviews and the delay or derailing of numerous projects. Admits a member of the state Board of Fisheries and Wildlife, "If species are kept on that list that don't meet current scientific standards, that puts in question the whole regulatory process."

The result of all this fancy footwork is artificially constricted

supply that drives housing and rental prices skyward, obliterat-
ing hope and impoverishing the lower classes, and pushing the
middle classes toward foreclosure or desperate out-of-state
flight. The lone beneficiaries: affluent property owners with the
disposable income to spend on lawyers and lobbying to keep
their true-blue wonderland nice and pristine. "If the residents
and businesses in greater Boston are seriously interested in making affordable housing a reality, they must lower the barriers
against new construction," concludes Glaeser. "Because the only
way to reduce the price of something is to produce more of it, it
is logically incoherent to be both an advocate of affordable housing and an opponent of new construction."

But logical coherence has never been a boomer concern, and
without that discipline, the high ground is rarely conceded.
Glaeser's findings were an invitation to "allow developers free
reign to pillage and plunder towns and exit with the profits,"
wrote David Pierotti of upscale Topsfield in an angry letter to the
Globe. "Perhaps the state could sell the Bunker Hill Monument
and Plymouth Rock to China to help us achieve our economic
potential. If the developers find the rules and regulations in Massachusetts too restrictive, perhaps Kansas might be more to their
liking."

As the ongoing outmigration of skilled workers, jobs, and
capital suggests, Pierotti's snotty suggestion—so reminiscent
of the send-Romney-back-to-Utah mantra of the 2002 state
Democratic Convention—is often gladly followed by those
with the means to escape. Less fortunate are the tens of thousands of poor, mostly nonwhite children trapped in cata-
strophically failing public schools. As part of a 1993 education

reform law that promised billions in new spending on teacher salaries and support, Massachusetts began allowing private groups to create charter schools free of union rules that too often stifle innovation and lock in failure. But despite waiting lists that run into the thousands for seats in the state's fifty-seven charter schools, the state's politically powerful teacher unions have fought to keep a cap on the number of charters with the same ferocity they manifest in fighting the dismissal or demotion of incompetent teachers. When the unions get called out for lying about charters not being public schools, their political sycophants step in with specious arguments about the "draining of resources" away from unionized schools, as if there was something immoral about tax dollars going to salvage the futures of the children of taxpayers. Meanwhile, surveys of public school parents have found runaway preference for the longer school days, better discipline, and more intensive instruction many charter schools offer. "I want to see parents be able to take control of the education of their own children," says Judy Burnette, a veteran activist for better educational opportunities for kids in her low-income, mainly black Boston neighborhood. "I'm sick of the system, sick of initiatives. People have just 12 to 14 years to educate their children, and that is not a lot of time."

But boomer teacher union leaders don't feel the urgency. The public schools are their backyard, and fresh ideas, energy, and hope are not welcome in it. In a cave-in to union pressure, half of the new charters created by a modest expansion a few years back were designated as union shops, or so-called Horace Mann charter schools. But when a coalition of union teachers in Fitchburg, an impoverished central Massachusetts city, tried to form a charter school, the head of the Fitchburg Teachers Association refused to let them go forward. "Too many unanswered questions," he explained. Said Nancy Bacon, a union teacher and co-organizer of the charter group, "One man held a school system, a school committee, and administration, and a town hostage to his whims." Given the chance to define reform on their own terms, Massachusetts teacher union leaders have made it clear they prefer to maintain a destructive, arguably racist status quo. Out of a potential forty-eight Horace Mann charters, only seven are operating, and there hasn't been a single new application in more than two years.

In her book *Singular Generation,* Wanda Urbanska noted the boomer propensity for designing self-justifying moral constructs, churches of one that require no compromise. "Sheilaism," she called it, named for a friend who "had this little voice inside" sending her a tidy, gratifying message: "God is whatever I feel."

If Sheila's on the money, then heavenly dispensation is readily at hand for Massachusetts boomer liberals who have perfected the art of fobbing off thinly veiled racism, classism, and self-serving NIMBYism as concerns over parking and traffic, historic preservation, environmentalism, and "protecting" the public schools. No wonder the likes of Michael Dukakis and John Kerry are greeted with such cynicism when they go national with their rhetoric of commitment to commonwealth. When I hear a local liberal rail against racial profiling by police, I reflexively think of the wealthy liberals of Brattle Street who were so quick to drop a dime on my teenage friend, and of Joan Wallace-Benjamin from the Commonwealth

Day School, trying to explain the inexplicable to her young son. "I don't know that surprise was necessarily my reaction to it," she recalled later, "as much as chagrin and disappointment that we really haven't come as far as we sometimes think we have."

CHAPTER TWELVE

....

What Hate Does

DID SARAH LOY really have to have her head slammed against the sidewalk so that gay marriage could march on in Massachusetts?

The distinctly unthreatening Loy, a twenty-seven-year-old brunette holding a handmade sign that read No Discrimination in the Constitution, was part of a group of about fifty same-sex marriage advocates who showed up to picket. Their target was a Worcester rally of backers of a proposed constitutional amendment overriding the state supreme court's 2003 legalization of gay marriage. A few weeks before, legislators adjourned a special session called to consider the gay-marriage ban, a move to run out the clock on the constitutional amendment process without ever having to vote on it. Accordingly, the focus of the rally was on outrage over the denial of a chance for the public to vote on a landmark, controversial new civil right imposed by a 4-to-3 vote of a state court. "I have never heard or seen anything like this in the history of Massachusetts," former Boston mayor and U.S. ambassador to the Vatican Ray Flynn told the crowd. "We're the same as Iraq. We're the same as Afghanistan. We're the same as Russia." "Four judges do not get to decide what sin is," added Larry Cirignano, like Flynn, an officer of Catholic Citizenship, a group formed to promote "pro-life, pro-family" political advocacy.

Perhaps Cirignano saw sin in the specter of Sarah Loy and her sign, some 30 feet away. There is no doubt that he saw red. According to eyewitness accounts and a criminal assault-and-battery complaint filed by Worcester police, as counterdemonstrators chanted, "You lost, go home, get over it," Cirignano charged from the podium into the crowd, grabbed Loy by both shoulders, and said, "You need to get out of here right now," before pushing her backward onto the sidewalk. Through her tears as she was helped to her feet, Loy yelled out, "That's what hate does."

On the state's liberal blogs, same-sex marriage supporters were beside themselves. "This confirms what most of us already know to be true," wrote Tom Lang, codirector of Know Thy Neighbor, a group famous for posting online the names and addresses of citizen signers of the initiative petition to ban gay marriage. "The anti-gay marriage activists only believe in democracy when it suits their religious agenda and not when it means protecting the civil rights of a minority." On Blue-MassGroup.com, a regular commentator posted a photo of Cardinal Sean O'Malley, head of the Boston archdiocese, posing with Larry Cirignano and Ray Flynn, and taunted the cardinal's anti-gay-marriage stance: "Gay sex is just sick! I mean anal penetration!? Eww. To you, it's sicker than soon-to-be babies being sucked out of tubes, right?"

Wielding a pickaxe where a bobby pin would suffice, this blogger reflects the unbridled venom of gay marriage supporters. "We would kill it with a handgun or a hand grenade," one Democratic state representative bluntly promised. Unsurprisingly, the vitriol is returned in kind by its targets, who argued that the 170,000 signatures they gathered shouldn't be so crudely dismissed. "On an issue as important as marriage, I think the people deserve a chance to vote," said Rich Sorcinelli, who had driven nearly two hours from West Springfield to protest. "Less than this has brought wars. This is what brings civil disobedience." Gay people, concluded Roberto Miranda, chairman of the petition drive, "portray themselves as victims, but in this case they act as oppressors."

As Rodney King famously asked amid the 3,600 fires, 10,000 arrests, and 60 fatalities of another seminal boom-era conflict, the 1992 Los Angeles riots, "Can't we all just get along?" The answer from boom-era Massachusetts is clear: no, we can't, not without court intervention that may impose legal solutions, but leaves badly needed social consensus starving for oxygen.

Controversy over judicial activism is nothing new. As Georgetown University law professor Peter Edelman points out, from Frankin Delano Roosevelt's judiciary bashing during his 1937 bid to pack the Supreme Court, through the right-wing's "Impeach Earl Warren" rhetoric in response to desegregation and criminals' rights rulings of the 1950s and beyond, judicial activism has been "a ubiquitous epithet . . . a scare phrase for either side to hurl at the other in place of a substantive argument that a particular judicial decision is wrong on its merits." But as the most litigious generation in history has asserted full control over the political culture, the war over judicial activism has escalated dramatically. The left applauded the "arrogance" of rulings like *Roe v. Wade* that drove the right wild. But as Edelman notes, "It is the liberals who now cry 'activism' when the court strikes down laws establishing gun-free school zones, set-asides for minority contractors, state damages for discrimination based on age or disability, civil remedies for violence against women, and citizen suits under the Endangered Species Act."

For the boomers, the perpetual tension between popular or legislative will and judicial authority isn't just political, it's personal, and the national political debate is littered with the resulting roadkill. When a string of violent attacks on judges made headlines in early 2005, conservative senator John Cornyn of Texas was quick to connect the dots. "I wonder whether there may be some connection between the perception . . . that judges are making political decisions—yet are unaccountable to the public—and the violence." This incendiary right-wing rhetoric has its overwrought response from the left. "Violence against judges is nothing short of domestic terrorism, and Cornyn (along with [Tom] DeLay and their ilk) are nothing more than apologists for such violence," wrote left-wing blogger Markos Moulitsas Zúniga of Daily Kos. "The GOP's war on the judiciary is now entering dangerous territory." And no single issue since abortion has fueled the

war over judicial activism more intensely than the Massachusetts gay-marriage law. George W. Bush pounced on the ruling
in his 2004 State of the Union address, decrying "activist
judges" redefining marriage "without regard for the will of the
people and their elected representatives." Ten months later,
eleven states passed anti-gay-marriage ballot initiatives, including Ohio, the state where yet another Democratic presidential
bid was lost.

It was jarring to see a Massachusetts legal precedent so emphatically rejected, given the state's illustrious history of populist legal activism. "A Common-wealth without lawes is like a
Ship without rigging and steeradge," was a common adage of
the mid-seventeenth century. The Salem witchcraft trials of
1692 marked a breakdown of justice, but were also notable for
the repentance that followed, including a public judicial apology. Back then, public involvement with the court system as
jurors, litigants, or witnesses was proportionally far more
widespread than today. "The high rate of participation in the
administration of justice . . . correlates to the growth of partic-
ipatory democracy," notes *The Encyclopedia of New England*.
Conflicts over tax and customs laws led to the Boston Tea Party
and the revolution that followed. Legal arguments for
colonists' rights were precedent for abolitionist distinctions between just and unjust laws over the next century. Emerson,
Thoreau, and other Massachusetts transcendentalists chafed at
the commercialism of the New World, but their advocacy for
reason over precedent led some to call the mid-nineteenth
century a time of "transcendentalization" of American law.
Post–Civil War legal thought was dominated by Massachusetts

thinkers—Oliver Wendell Holmes tying legal evolution to history and the political process rather than "natural law," and Louis Brandeis reminding courts of the sociological impact of their decisions.

But in the boomer era, Massachusetts has offered a distinctly less impressive model for the nation of an addictive overreliance on judicial activism at the expense of building popular support for social change. Boston's court-ordered desegregation turned out to be a tragic oxymoron, as Judge Garrity's ham-handed social engineering resulted in dramatic white flight, a near collapse of the city's middle-class core, and a school system more grotesquely segregated than ever before. A boomer lawyer who stepped in feces on a Boston Harbor beach in 1982 sued to force long-overdue government compliance with the federal Clean Water Act. The ensuing federal court-ordered cleanup produced the highest water and sewer rates in the country and sparked mass protests that included water-bill burning, an ironic new take on the anti–Vietnam War protests of local boomers' pre-homeowning days. In the end, the cleanup cost taxpayers $4.1 billion, but harbor beaches frequented by working-class residents still close often during the height of the summer due to pollution levels. Massachusetts's most recent pushing of the envelope is a state lawsuit against the federal Environmental Protection Agency trying to mandate by court order the vehicle emission standards that the legislative and executive branches have rejected. After all, argued the state attorney general, the verdict was in as far as boomer leadership is concerned: "Global warming is the most pressing environmental issue of our time."

Do the ends justify the means? Watching the Bush administration's foreign and counterterrorism policies unfold since
September 11 and the frog march forward of gay marriage
in Massachusetts over the same period, it seems both right-
and left-wing boomers have concluded they do. For boomer
George W. Bush and his followers, the niceties of process,
compromise, and the popular consensus they can generate are
an afterthought to prosecuting the war. Likewise, for boomer
Cheryl Jacques, former head of the Human Rights Campaign,
the Washington-based gay rights lobby, and for the gay marriage movement in Massachusetts, the very thought of their
newly minted marital right being put to a popular vote is an
abomination. "As Dr. Martin Luther King said, there is no
convenient time when the country will be comfortable with the
idea of full equality," she says.

Jacques, the former Massachusetts state senator who lost
that 2001 congressional race with her overemphasis on abortion, knows something about how comfortable her neighbors
are with gay people. Elected to the state legislature in the late
1980s from Needham, a liberal Boston suburb bordering Route
128, Jacques came out publicly as a lesbian in June 2000, in the
middle of an ugly squabble over the state's role in protecting
gay public school students from abuse. She and other Beacon
Hill liberals had fought off proposed funding cuts for gay-
themed student outreach, and in an op-ed column in the
Globe, Jacques wrote, "As a gay person myself, I understand
in a very personal way the tremendous pressure these young
people feel."

The day after the article appeared, Jacques attended a

ceremony in a relatively conservative corner of her district for
World War II veterans who had missed their high-school grad-
uations because of their service. On the way there, she worried
about the greeting she might receive from one veteran she
knew, a guy she called "the Candy Man" because whenever
they met, he would hand her a Hershey's Kiss and jokingly ask
her for a date. "There was a line of veterans seated in front, and
I thought, well, I bet some of them won't shake," Jacques told
me. But they did, some hugging her, others offering supportive
comments. Finally, she reached the Candy Man, who em-
braced Jacques, slipped her a Kiss, and whispered in her ear,
"Does this mean I don't have a chance with you?"

Jacques was easily reelected later that year, just as openly
gay Massachusetts congressmen Barney Frank and Gerry
Studds had been supported by their blue-collar constituencies
even after each man suffered through public scandals related
to their sexuality during the 1980s. Even the chairman of the
Republican State Committee appealed for Jacques's sexuality
to be out-of-bounds during the campaign. If anything, the remaining vestiges of homophobia in state politics were in the
Democratic Party, where devoutly Catholic legislators who
might otherwise be counted on to support progressive causes
were reluctant to back gay rights bills. But by the end of the
1990s, it was obvious that public tolerance had outpaced that of
the political culture. Boston's most popular radio talk-show
host, David Brudnoy, came out in 1994 during a hospitalization
for AIDS-related illness, and was overwhelmed with support
from his large conservative following. Susan Tracy, a closeted
lesbian during three terms as a state representative from a

staunchly Catholic neighborhood of Boston, came out during a
1998 run for Congress to widespread support among socially
conservative neighbors. "I found that people just don't care," she
said. "People judge you by who you are."

There's no evidence that the onset of gay marriage has done
anything but reaffirm that broad social tolerance in Massachusetts. It's tougher sledding elsewhere, even though a national
poll in 2006 as Republicans were gearing up to push for a vote
on a federal "defense of marriage" amendment found voters
placing gay marriage dead last on their issue priority list, trail-
ing everything from ethics reform to American flag–burning.
In Massachusetts, local polling has consistently shown strong
majority support for letting the law stand. No one in the legislature has lost their seat for supporting same-sex marriage;
meanwhile, five opponents of the law who made it a central issue in their campaigns were defeated. In the wake of a 2006
state election where pro-gay-marriage candidates ran the table,
2008 would seem a perfect opportunity to take on the predom-
inantly out-of-state forces behind gay-marriage repeal and, by
crushing them at the polls, snuff out once and for all the argument that same-sex marriage is merely a construct of liberal judicial fiat. "By denying the voters the chance to have the final
decision on marriage rights, the pro-marriage forces have lost
a clear chance at democratic legitimacy," wrote pro-gay-
marriage blogger Andrew Sullivan after the November 2006
adjournment on Beacon Hill. "Yes, in some respects, civil
rights should not be up for a vote. But many opponents of
equality in marriage do not accept the premise that civil marriage is a civil right for gays. I think they're wrong; but it's an

honest disagreement. And they're not wrong that equality in civil marriage is also a social change that should have democratic input. To prevent such input by parliamentary maneuvers taints the victory. I think we would have won the vote in 2008. I'm sorry we won't now get the chance to prove it."

Yet the local opposition to ratification of gay marriage by the voters remains adamant. The 170,000 signatures on the anti-gay-marriage petition represent "a groundswell of fraud and deceit, not of voter insistence," says Arline Isaacson of the Massachusetts Gay and Lesbian Political Caucus. And while boomer Susan Ryan-Vollmer, the editor of Boston's leading gay newspaper, *Bay Windows*, acknowledges that "we've moved past the point where lawmakers are afraid of supporting gay rights and gay marriage," and concedes that voter approval of gay marriage "would be a huge victory," she still prefers to see the measure killed in the back rooms of Beacon Hill. Why? "Fear," she says. "I don't understand it, but it's fear."

What is she afraid of? Not the voters, but the same political culture that so reflexively punts to the courts to avoid the hard work of building grassroots support for social change. Even in their securely blue political paradise, the Democrats who dominate the Massachusetts political culture have provided "very little to almost no leadership on marriage equality," Ryan-Vollmer says. What else is new? Ending public school segregation. Clean water. Clean air. All laudable goals with potentially broad public support. But boomer political leadership repeatedly fails to take on those issues, then defers to the judicial branch for often ham-handed imposition of their agenda. For liberals so profoundly imbued with a sense of their own moral rightness, and so personally invested in making everyone else fall in line, the timidity of this approach is striking. Worse, the damage it sometimes wreaks on progressive causes is palpable. How much agony might the nation have been spared—and how diminished might the pro-life movement now be—if a woman's right to choose had been established via the legislative process, one state at a time, instead of by judicial order? The transformative social effects of the Civil Rights Act of 1964, the product of patient, difficult coalition building and persuasion, are apparent to all; no honest observers make the same claims of the school-busing fiascos in Boston, Detroit, or Charlotte.

The sorry truth is, the political elites of Kennedy country don't especially trust the judgment of their flock. "The pols own the government here, it's theirs, and when we try to talk back to them, they feel under siege," says Barbara Anderson, the antitax veteran of nearly three decades of local referendum drives and grassroots activism. "The us-versus-them mentality is much stronger here than anywhere else I've seen. Even the Republicans, if they have to choose between us and their insider pals, they choose their pals." Anderson and her group, Citizens for Limited Taxation and Government, broke even on their two biggest crusades, winning their 1980 property-tax limitation drive, losing a 1990 attempt to roll back state taxes (in the same year that a tax-cutting Republican was elected governor). Voter prudence and moderation were in evidence both times, and unlike California, where the initiative petition process has long since mushroomed out of control, in Massachusetts the ballots routinely include only a handful of referendum questions. Yet as the boomers have taken control of Beacon Hill, considerable energy has been spent on neutering the initiative petition process. Within the last decade, voters by wide margins have approved a tax deduction to spur charitable giving, a "clean elections" system of providing public financing for political candidates, and a rollback of the income tax to 5 percent. All three were ignored by legislators. In 2005, the legislature nearly passed a bill placing draconian restrictions on the petition signature-gathering process. It took a bipartisan coalition ranging from the left-wing Massachusetts Public Interest Research Group, a Ralph Nader creation, to the right-wing Massachusetts Family Institute, the group sponsoring the gay-marriage repeal, to rally successful opposition to the measure.

"It's dead," says Barbara Anderson of the citizen petition process. "Why would you go out and get signatures when they're just going to blow you off anyway? All you have left is the two-party system, and we really don't have much of one anymore. This is what happens when you get any kind of absolute ascendancy. As soon as they get locked in, they become the problem."

From the other end of the political spectrum, Susan Ryan-Vollmer offers a similar analysis. Even gay lobbyists who had spent years fighting for gay rights on Beacon Hill were reluctant to push for same-sex marriage when it became a live prospect early in the decade, she claims. "They did not like this grassroots uprising; they wanted to control everything." In this case, boomer leadership combines three spectacularly antidemocratic traits—a chronic lack of confidence in the people, overweening confidence in their own correctness, and a willingness to risk ugly fallout by using the courts to accomplish through judicial power what they could not through the legislative process. Out of concern for the future of her own marriage, Ryan-Vollmer endorses legislative deep-sixing of the gay marriage–repeal petition, but not for reasons flattering to anti-repeal legislators and lobbyists. A 2008 referendum campaign, no matter how tolerant the Massachusetts electorate seems toward same-sex marriage, is "the last thing we want" because it would be micromanaged by those same political elites, and she observes, "They are completely capable of fucking it up."

This attitude may prove a bad break for gay couples elsewhere who find their local progress toward marital rights hampered by a backlash against judicial intervention that gives cover to homophobes and pause to moderates. Thirty-one states already elect at least some of their judges, and pressure to rein in the courts is building. The Justice at Stake Campaign, a pet project of left-wing political financier George Soros, calls 2006 "the most threatening election yet for fair and impartial courts. . . . Misleading and partisan attacks on judges' decisions are bringing politics into the courtroom."

Heaven forbid. And woe be unto the Massachusetts politician who dares suggest a more conciliatory approach. Gay marriage "may be gaining some level of public acceptance, but it will not go away without giving the voters an opportunity to agree or disagree with the Supreme Judicial Court's opinion," wrote Democratic state senator Richard Moore, a supporter of domestic benefits for gay couples, in a published commentary after the November 2006 mugging of the repeal petition. To which blog poster jconway wrote on the liberal Blue Mass Group Web site, amid a general hammering of Moore, "Give me a break, a majority cannot vote on the rights of a minority, that's not democracy!"

A democracy with no more majority rule or honest voter initiative process? Only a boomer could stake such a claim so righteously and without irony. Lee Swislow of Gay and Lesbian Advocates and Defenders cited the generation's favorite rationalization in her call for the legislature to continue dodging a direct vote on the gay-marriage repeal petition, even after the supreme judicial court ruled the maneuver unconstitutional. Said Swislow, "This is my right to marry the person I love, and putting that on the ballot feels like the most cynical thing that could happen, on a very personal level." Gay and lesbian couples can't be faulted for pulling out all stops to protect a cherished right. But rule by judicial fiat can and does backfire. The scolding of the legislature's behavior by the supreme judicial court—the same court that legalized gay marriage in the first place—alarmed enough legislators to produce a vote in January 2007, allowing the repeal petition to move forward. The move came over the objections of the likes of state senator Ed Augustus, who argued for killing the petition with a procedural vote on the grounds that "Massachusetts has always been the conscience of the nation, that is our role."

It's a conscience that's guilty of causing nasty political fallout. When a federal judge tried to ban snowmobiling in Yellowstone National Park a few years back, the blistering and successful pushback included this post to a conservative Web site: "Judge Sullivan disagrees with the Park Service's conclusions drawn

from certain studies. Well, then turn in your robe and go work
for the Park Service, you ass. What are we paying these bureaucrats for when regulatory judgments are adequately carried out
by judicial fiat?"

Harsh words, assaulting a vital democratic institution. As
Sarah Loy might put it, "That's what hate does."

CHAPTER THIRTEEN

....

The Two Massachusettses

KICKING BACK WITH the *Sunday Globe* on December 10, 2006, you could easily conclude that Massachusetts was a fantastic place to live.

What a view from the gleaming new Regatta Riverview Residences on the Boston-Cambridge line, a display ad in the real estate section shows. From your picture window, there's the gentle curve of the Charles River, with the world-class Massachusetts General Hospital complex giving way to newly renovated parks along the water's edge. It's an easy walk or bike ride along the river to the beautifully restored Hatch Shell to hear the Boston Pops play during the summer. In winter, a snowfall makes the colonial-era buildings on Beacon Hill look like a Currier and Ives drawing. Top-shelf shopping—Gucci, Tiffany, Barneys, and Saks—is an easy walk away on New-bury Street or at the Copley Place mall. But why go out? The

Globe ad for Regatta Riverview cites a private theater, fitness center, indoor pool, valet parking, and twenty-four-hour concierge, and notes, "With all of these amenities, there's no excuse not to buy." (Unless, that is, you can't come up with the cool million it might take to snag a two-bedroom unit.)

Perhaps a low-interest loan can be arranged through the college or university you might well be working for if you're condo shopping there. Two-thirds of page 1 above the fold is taken up by color photos of gleaming new residential and research facilities proposed for local campuses; the headline reads, "Major Projects for Area Colleges Expected to Boost Landscape, Economy." The construction boom promises to spur creation of thousands of new jobs; the Massachusetts Institute of Technology's new cancer research center alone is expected to house more than four hundred engineers and biologists and their support staffs.

Don't worry, those jobs will pay well. At Boston University, where a year at full tuition costs more than $44,000 (not counting books and personal expenses), they're rolling in dough and making sure it stays that way by sparing no expense in the white-hot competition for well-heeled students. An expansive *Globe* spread across the front of the city-and-region section shows white-jacketed Asian women preparing student meals to order on a Mongolian grill at one gleaming new student cafeteria. Freshman Mark Marchant from Florida says he loves his mom's cooking, but he "can't wait" to hit the Warren Towers dining hall for the lavish omelettes, fresh salads, and yummy baked ziti. And when the 'rents come in for homecoming weekend, they can take you out to dinner at one of the dozens of trendy spots in one of the nation's most acclaimed restaurant cities.

Other places may offer some of the above, but Boston has something extra: progressive brain power. On page A3 of the *Globe*, the weekly "Observer" details the verbal and intellectual mastery of newly elected governor Deval Patrick as he led his team to victory in Harvard Law School's ultraprestigious Ames Moot Court competition in 1981. While the nation contemplates taking a chance on Barack Obama, an erudite black Harvard Law grad, we've already taken the plunge with our own mini-Obama. The *Globe's* ideas section leads with a lengthy piece about how Patrick intends not merely to govern, but "has spoken eloquently of reengaging citizens and reinvigorating our democracy." Inside on the letters-to-the-editor page, a recent op-ed article defending the pharmaceutical industry as an engine of medical innovation is being reassuringly dismembered by not just one, but three former editors-in-chief of the *New England Journal of Medicine.* "Industry R & D consists largely of clinical trials that often serve marketing objectives more than medical science," they write. "Most truly innovative drugs stem from publicly funded research done in government and industry labs." Or one of the high lifestyle–supporting new university labs growing like kudzu here in Collegetown, USA. After a long week of fighting off the red tide of big pharma, beleaguered Bostonians have their pick of ideologically reassuring diversions. Left-wing comedian Jimmy Tingle's "politically charged one-man show" *American Dream* is in residence in Somerville, and over at Harvard's Fogg Art Museum there's a display of ephemera celebrating "politically adversarial sentiments," including a "demonic" Andy Warhol portrait of Richard Nixon with a "scary green face" and a red T-shirt with an image of George W. Bush over the words "Blame Yale." (Curiously, given the setting, the exhibit is entitled "Dissent.")

Yes, it's the best of times to be living in the bluest state—if you're loaded with disposable income from one of our choice health-care or education or financial services jobs. But Massachusetts is really two states. And there are some other stories in this morning's paper that bode ill if you're luckless enough to live in the one without the matchless Charles River view.

The incoming Boston police commissioner says he's concerned that residents of Roxbury and Mission Hill, low-income neighborhoods of color far from the twinkling lights of downtown, wait significantly longer for police to respond to 911 calls because of the heavy volume of violent emergencies. There's an item about six experienced, high-ranking managers of the public transit system, all earning from $69,000 to $82,000 a year, being fired for allegedly showing up hours late for work and cutting out early on their shifts, falsifying work logs and time sheets to cover up, at a time when subway and bus fares are about to soar because of the transit system's huge budget deficit. The upscale condo market may be booming, but middle-class homeowners are caught in a nasty real estate downturn; statewide, the median sales price of a single-family home has dropped more than 4 percent in a year, home sales have collapsed, and foreclosures are skyrocketing.

And most troubling of all is the *Globe*'s other lead page 1 story, right alongside its bouquet to university expansionism.

"Bay State's Labor Force Diminishing," reads the headline, and the facts, from a labor-market study by the nonpartisan Massachusetts Institute for a New Commonwealth (MINC), are frightening if you're on the outside of the Regatta Riverview Residences looking in.

Even in the aging, high-cost Northeast, where most states have trailed the decade's national recovery, Massachusetts stands out as an economic black hole. From 2003 to 2005, the Massachusetts labor force shrank by nearly 2 percent; it was the only state labor force to decline each year at a time when the national labor force was growing by more than 3 percent. Skilled, educated workers aren't coming to Massachusetts, or perhaps they're being trampled at the border by the droves of younger workers with families—workers in their prime working years—rushing to get out. They're heading to warm-weather, high-growth, low-tax magnets like Florida and Texas, as well as to high-tax frost-belt places like Connecticut and Rhode Island where the cost of living is marginally more bearable. While Massachusetts boasts the highest percentage (32.9%) of working-age residents with a bachelor's or higher degree, it is also hemorrhaging well-educated workers. In 2004, a total of 18,000 people with a bachelor's degree or better fled for greener pastures.

The drying-up of the labor pool, especially workers with superior skills and education, "tends to make a place less attractive and deters employers from opening new facilities or expanding existing operations," the MINC study notes. Yet there's an apparent anomaly here. The skilled Massachusetts workforce has been its calling card for decades, the state's vaunted "competitive advantage." As recently as the latter part of the 1990s, the state economy was considered robust, even though the labor force was nearly as stagnant then as it is now. The Massachusetts economy expanded during the nineties primarily by ratcheting up labor productivity to the third-highest rate in the nation. But "the prosperity of this decade was not widely shared," the MassInc study finds. "The gains went disproportionately to those families with the highest incomes. An economy based on increasing productivity clearly had success, but it is somewhat risky to be solely dependent on increased productivity for economic success, particularly for achieving a broad-based prosperity."

Who missed out? For the most part, working-class men without college degrees, who are dramatically less evident in the Massachusetts labor force now than at the start of the 1990s. The exodus of the manufacturing economy for more fertile turf in the South, the West, and foreign countries has been ongoing in Massachusetts since at least the 1940s, and politicians and policy makers here have been buzzing about its implications ever since, with little apparent effect. The jobs that blue-collar men could make a living at disappeared. Most of the remaining opportunities for workers with limited education were in fields already dominated by women, such as retail and health care. Even with a high-school diploma, pickings became sparse for young Massachusetts men; for high-school dropouts, few places in America were bleaker. Less than 32 percent of the state's high-school dropouts have any kind of job, the sixth-lowest ranking among the fifty states. Concludes the MINC study: "The withdrawal of men with limited education has implications for family formation, including a rise in single-parent families. In addition, their withdrawal has contributed to higher levels of income inequality and increased dependency on state and federal aid. . . . The continuing withdrawal of men from the state's labor force signals a serious and growing mismatch between workers and jobs. These challenges appear to be the most severe in the state's large urban centers, such as Boston, Springfield, Lawrence, Fall River, and New Bedford."

Who's making a serious effort to meet those challenges through the progressive populism the bluest state supposedly embodies? Ted Kennedy keeps the federal aid flowing as best he can, with the help of a few diligent congressmen. A smattering of altruistic nonprofits and civic-minded corporations pitch in. But it's telling that whenever pollsters ask Massachusetts residents which local political leader they respect the most, neither Ted nor any big-name boomer pol gets the nod.

WHEN I VISIT the most popular politician in Massachusetts at his office on his sixty-fourth birthday, the staff has surprised him with a cake with his favorite saying written in icing across the top: "Who cares?" It's an example of his skepticism toward fancy titles and grandiose claims, and the built-in bullshit detector that often leads him to suffer pompous fools ungraciously. And even though he diplomatically refuses to name names, it's clear that he places much of the state's boomer leadership in that category. "It's really lost its focus," he says.

He was born in 1942, close enough to the vague generational

dividing line to be considered a cusp boomer. But while he holds an array of positions in common with liberal boomer elites—staunch support of gun control, gay marriage, needle exchange, and increased aid to the homeless, to name a few—he is an anachronism in every other way. There is nothing entitled or pedigreed about him. His degrees are from an obscure junior college and a public commuter university. The son of Italian immigrants in a blue-collar Boston neighborhood, he lives there still in the same ultramodest six-room Cape he's owned for decades. The family's fourteen-year-old Ford Taurus only recently bit the dust. His son, a police detective, makes more than he does. His lifestyle frills include a semiregular round on the city-owned golf course and an occasional trip to Italy or Ireland. A grueling, seven-days-a-week work schedule that usually begins before dawn and ends long after dark doesn't allow time for much else. Even if he wanted to sleep in once in a while, the phone wouldn't allow it. He lists his home phone number in the white pages, and it's not some secondary line that dumps callers directly into voice mail. People know that if they call it during those brief windows when he's at home, chances are he'll answer himself, although if you're a fool, look out. "In this business, you can get insulated if you don't talk to people," he says. "When that happens, people get caught up in their own importance."

It's a trap that has ensnared a laundry list of the state's top boomer politicians, from Michael Dukakis to John Kerry to Mitt Romney, all ducking out on their local obligations to bestow their priceless gifts on the nation, and the most popular politician in Massachusetts can't fathom it. "You know what drives most pols? Getting their name in the paper. But it's not about you, it's about why you're there. Who you're serving. Why can't you do the best job you can in the position you have?" he wonders. "People get into office and automatically they're thinking, 'What's my next job?' There's no commitment. I think that's why people trust me; I've never looked to move up. I believe this is a contract with the voters. They put me here—I have to do a good job for them."

Boomers and broken contracts seem to go together like a tasteful wine-food pairing on the menu of the bistros they like to frequent. From the Gingrich-era Contract with America to the bipartisan promises of social security, health-care, and campaign finance reform, conservative and liberal boomers alike have specialized in sweeping visions that somehow are never quite realized (or, as in the case of the Big Dig, consummated with appalling costs and consequences). How ironic that the most popular politician in Massachusetts regularly takes heat from boomer pundits and pols for failing to make grandiose promises. "If there is a vision for the next term, it's not yet apparent," wrote a *Boston Herald* columnist on the eve of his landslide reelection to a third term. Added a *Globe* columnist, "If there is a vision, it needs rearticulation and readjustment."

"I don't like the word 'vision,'" says our man, but because of a chronic speech impediment, you have to work a bit to make it out. This defect is a source of much amusement for many of his more articulate boomer peers, who snicker about his garbled syntax behind his back even as they chafe at the sight of his sky-high approval ratings. His achievements—new housing and commercial development in long-neglected black and Latino neighborhoods, a restructuring of the local health-care infrastructure that stabilized services to the low-income population, the start of long-term improvements in the wretched public school system—aren't the kinds of things the critics see on their drive to work. But since he, unlike most of the critics, actually lives among the people they write and chatter about, he's confident in his take on what they really want from him. "Education, housing, crime, it's really a quality of life thing," he says. "Your dream is that a young couple can walk down to the playground and there's no broken glass there, the husband can get a good job [how heteronormative!], and the kid can go off to a good school. Then, at night, you can have a good time right in the neighborhood because the neighborhood is strong." And when the chattering classes describe their vision of the state's most pressing future needs, it's a sure bet they don't include his top priority—more land for expansion by the health-care industry, one of the region's few healthy economic sectors. "Where do they grow?" he asks. "I'm concerned about what'll happen after I'm gone."

While the stutter-free boomer graduates of blue-chip colleges mock his supposedly stunted foresight, he wonders what on earth they're doing right here and now. "There's no economic plan for Massachusetts, nobody's thought about it," he says. "What's our state slogan, anyway?" (Pathetically, it's Massachusetts—Make It Yours, but the story gets worse. That anemic motto was created by an ad agency after hundreds of citizens sent in their own suggestions, some of them sarcastic, such as Massachusetts: Lower Taxes than Sweden. The chosen slogan was as close as tourism officials, demoralized by a sharp downturn in that once-booming local industry, dared come to the confident pitch of the late 1970s: You Can Make It in Massachusetts.) "People keep promising us, but where's the action? We in Massachusetts sit here like big executives waiting for business to come to us, and it isn't happening." Meanwhile, he sees boomer hubris and entitlement devouring the seed corn at a prolific rate. Unionized public employees paying only 10 percent of their health insurance while public sector costs have soared by more than 90 percent in just the past five years. NIMBY activists squeezing the revenue base by shooting down desperately needed development. Grotesque underfunding of community colleges that in turn fail to graduate even a third of their students. "They don't want to look at the folks who need that to move up," he says disgustedly.

He mentions the increasingly desperate fight to keep blue-chip employers like Fidelity Investments, one of the state's largest providers of plum white-collar jobs, from bolting for lower-cost oases. Massachusetts passed a modest sales-tax break for mutual funds a decade ago to keep Fidelity here, but ever since, while the legislature's been napping, competitors have been pilfering those jobs at a prolific rate. In 2005, Rhode Island rewrote its income-tax laws to exempt part of employee bonuses and give breaks to high-wage workers from large companies that promise to expand their local workforce. Shortly thereafter, Fidelity shipped 1200 jobs a short drive down I-95. The tax break was only part of the picture; company executives cited far lower housing prices, consumer prices, and health-care costs. "We need to focus even more sharply on the economics of our business," said Fidelity's chief financial officer. But a year later, in a debate among the three Democratic candidates for governor, it was clear that Massachusetts's liberal leadership hadn't gotten the message. None of the three would even consider similar tax breaks to keep a major employer here. "But I do think that we have to be much more robust partners with Massachusetts businesses to encourage them to stay here and to grow here," was the vague offering of Deval Patrick, the eventual winner.

Then there's the Big Dig, the $15 billion death trap our man watched being carelessly built from his office window. For less than half the amount spent on getting the professional classes to the airport more quickly and hiding downtown traffic underground, Massachusetts could have housed every homeless person, fed every hungry child, and built a world-class public transit system, he acknowledges. "We could have done that, but we had a priority of removing the Central Artery," he says, shaking his head in dismay. Why have Massachusetts elites—the boomer liberals weaned on a vow to instill progressive priorities in the government they control—done such a poor job of addressing the real needs of the people they claim to champion? "They can't see it, they can't touch it," he says. "They can't feel it."

It's not just boomer Beacon Hill that disappoints and infuriates him. "There's a total lack of leadership in Washington," he says. "They're too focused on Democrats versus Republicans, not on what is the common good." And it appalls him that back at home, obsessive partisans at times try to impede him from doing what he thinks is best for his constituents. "Some Republicans have good ideas," he says. "I get criticized by some of my fellow Democrats when I try to work with them. I'm not going to talk to someone who might be able to help me because he's a Republican? That's how small-minded we are. Give me a break."

Sound familiar? It shouldn't come as a surprise that the most popular politician in Massachusetts is the mayor of Boston, Tom Menino. Warts, speech impediment, and all, Menino actually delivers on many of the promises that his boomer contemporaries just talk about. At the other end of the boom generation from Rob Dolan, the Generation X mayor of Melrose, Menino shares Dolan's contempt for and impatience with the narcissistic meanderings of the state's boomer leadership and Democratic partisans, and their me-first constituencies. "It's not about us, it's about me, what can we do for my political benefit," he says.

By the time I graduated from Brandeis University (alma mater of Angela Davis and Abbie Hoffman) in 1977, that phrase was one of the received wisdoms of political life in the liberal capital of the most liberal state in the country, right up there along with "War is not healthy for children and other living things."

What did "The personal is political" really mean? Nobody in my circle knew for sure. But that didn't prevent us from taking it seriously. Thirty years later, some of my contemporaries in academia with time to spare still argue about who coined the phrase. Was it sociologist C. Wright Mills? Birth control activist Margaret Sanger? Radical feminist Carol Hanisch? (If it was her, were in trouble, because Hanisch also claims, "Personal problems are political problems. There are no personal solutions at this time.")

Years later, Googling the slogan, I found the consensus meaning of "The personal is political": the "broad texture and character" of our personal lives are not a result of our personalities and life choices, but are "defined by the broader political and social setting." We are what a corrupt political system makes us, and thus we suffer from "a totality of oppressions." It's a wonder, given Hanisch's depressing no-exit spin on this, that we even get out of bed.

But my peers in Cambridge didn't have quite the same gloomy, humbling take on it. "The personal is political" was a slogan from heaven for my generation, endowed with limitless self-esteem by our parents, instinctively understanding that the center of the universe looks back at us from the mirror every morning. We took it as a green light to let our gut feelings and personal biases—often mistaken for moral principles—dictate our civic behavior. We used it to justify a new brand of politics that valued personal identity over communal interests, all the while insisting they were one and the same. Widespread protests in the streets of Cambridge during the spring of 1970 were described as antiwar, but they were really a convention of grievances from feminists to anti-Zionists and everything in between. The uniform of choice that spring was a T-shirt with a red fist on the back, a generic but satisfyingly defiant symbol. Exotic concepts of discrimination with made-up names like "lookism," and "heteronorming" got their start from "The personal is political" and its comforting premise that if you believe strongly enough in your own oppression, just as the children in *Peter Pan* believed in fairies, it must be real.

What a boon to young thinkers without much knowledge

or maturity, but with strong feelings to spare. Because you felt it deep within your teenage soul, it was real and politically significant. Vietnam was the big issue. Civil rights, of course. But anything that affected you personally was likely to move quickly up the priority list. I recall pitched battles over the right to stage loud rock concerts on the Common on Sunday afternoons, bicyclists' rights, and just about anything else that pitted us against The Man, like the time we lay down in front of bulldozers to stop the destruction of a local park, an encounter advertised on handbills as "People's Park East." Our favorite book of 1970: Charles Reich's *The Greening of America,* with its self-affirming subtitle *How the Youth Revolution Is Trying to Make America Livable.* (Boomers to Greatest Generation: thanks for nothing.) "Politics was no longer simply a pocketbook issue but a moral issue as well, subject to moral imperatives and moral absolutes," recalls Sen. Barack Obama in *The Audacity of Hope.* "Politics was decidedly personal, insinuating itself into every interaction—whether between black and white, men and women—and implicating itself in every assertion or rejection of authority. . . . The arguments of the era were understood not simply as political disputes but as individual choices that defined personal identity and moral standing."

There are those who deride the politicization of the personal as the masturbatory narcissism of the Me Generation, an elevation of self at the expense of consensus, compromise, and community. It's a criticism Massachusetts boomers are easily insulated from—we don't much go for Fox News or the *Wall Street Journal.* National Public Radio's "Morning Edition," airing simultaneously on no less than two Boston FM stations, draws huge drive-time numbers, while Pastor Perry Lockwood, in his seventieth year of caring "for the lost multitudes on the way to hell," goes unnoticed on a 5,000-watt AM station.

But even here in the citadel of liberal groupthink, some consequences of this boomer credo have been unwelcome. Massachusetts liberals recoiled in horror in the 1980s, when conservative boomers got hip to our favorite slogan and aggressively placed their religious and moral convictions at the center of their political agenda. We are aghast at the political fervor of pro-life zealots, and are one of only three states to require a restraining "bubble zone" around patients outside abortion clinics to separate them from the protestors. The sheer intensity of the self-righteousness on both sides when liberal and conservative boomers clash has been well-documented as has the egregiously partisan, uncompromising political climate it yields. This shouldn't come as a surprise. When your politics and your inner self are joined at the hip, quarrels over policy aren't just the give-and-take of a civil democracy. They're fighting words. For all of our rhetoric about creating a new kind of open-minded politics superior to the turf-conscious ward-heeling of our elders, we are quick to go postal when someone challenges our most intimate political assumptions. For boomer George W. Bush, this translates into Don't Mess with Texas. For his liberal counterparts in my home state it might as well be Don't Screw with the Kennedys.

What could be more personal—and a higher priority— than a boomer's self-aggrandizement? The selfishness and self-delusion that Menino and Dolan see from their patches of the Massachusetts grassroots should be profoundly troubling to future boomer leadership both locally and nationally. A recent Harris poll found that while 51 percent of boomers see themselves as "open to new ideas," only 12 percent of nonboomers see them that way. There's reason to believe that this generational myopia and the debate over how to move beyond it will be a key element of the 2008 presidential race. After all, Hillary Clinton could have been talking about modern-day Massachusetts when she stressed, in her 1969 Wellesley College graduation speech, the importance of "that mutuality of respect between people where you don't see people as percentage points. Where you don't manipulate people. Where you're not interested in social engineering for people. The struggle for an integrated life existing in an atmosphere of communal trust and respect is one with desperately important political and social consequences."

More recently, Barack Obama has observed that "in the back and forth between Clinton and Gingrich, and in the elections of 2000 and 2004, I sometimes felt as if I were watching the psychodrama of the Baby Boom generation—a tale rooted in old grudges and revenge plots hatched on a handful of college campuses long ago—played out on the national stage. The victories that the sixties generation brought about—the admission of minorities and women into full citizenship, the strengthening of individual liberties and the healthy willingness to question authority—have made Amerca a far better place for all its citizens. But what has been lost in the process, and has yet to be replaced, are those shared assumptions—that quality of trust and fellow feeling—that brings us together as Americans." Gingrich himself shares that discontent with

boomer progress. "I don't think we've quite crossed the thresh-
old yet of understanding how hard history is," he told me in a
recent interview. "The boomers inherited a lot, and now we're
actually going to have to roll up our sleeves and earn the next
act."

Linda Greenhouse had it partly right. In June 2006, the
New York Times's Supreme Court reporter gave a speech at
Harvard's Radcliffe Institute describing how she lost it at a recent Simon and Garfunkel concert. Sitting in the darkened
arena surrounded by thousands of aging boomers like herself,
Greenhouse recalled the political idealism of her Cambridge
college days in the late 1960s, and her youthful commitment to
civil rights, women's rights, and antiwar activism. "We were
absolutely united in one conviction: the belief that in future
decades, if the world lasted that long, when our turn came to
run the country, we wouldn't make the same mistakes. Our
generation would do a better job. I cried that night in the Simon and Garfunkel concert out of the realization that my faith
had been misplaced. We were not doing a better job. We had
not learned from the old mistakes. Our generation had not
proved to be the solution. We were the problem."

Predictably, with the patented tunnel vision of her generation, Greenhouse defines "we" as the conservative perpetrators
of "the sustained assault on women's reproductive freedom
and the hijacking of public policy by religious fundamental-
ism," among other offenses. Standing at the epicenter of the
Massachusetts boomer fiasco, she cannot, or will not, look
around and see egregious liberal failures. Thus, you should not
hold your breath waiting for the likes of John Edwards to in-

terrupt one of his patented discourses on "the two Americas" during the 2008 campaign to explain how it is that the very same ego-driven neglect of true economic fairness and social justice he decries on the right is thriving like a flesh-eating virus right here in the bluest state of all.

CHAPTER FOURTEEN

....

"Boston, We Have a Problem"

PERHAPS, AS TED KENNEDY put it when he conceded the end of his only presidential campaign at the 1980 Democratic Convention, "The work goes on, the cause endures, the hope still lives, and the dream shall never die." But here in Kennedy country, for the working people American liberalism has long sworn allegiance to, the dream is on life support. Walking around the July 2004 Democratic National Convention in Boston, with George W. Bush already well into the downward spiral that opened the door for a Democratic Congress two years later, it was hard for me not to trip over some of the reasons why.

Behind a cluster of TV lights and gawkers, it's the Rev. Jesse Jackson, denouncing Bush for "carrying a grudge" against Saddam Hussein. A young woman about one-third Jackson's age passes by the scrum and asks, "Who is that old guy?" Told it's the man once widely known as the president of black America, she looks puzzled. "I never heard of him. Who is he again?"

A few yards away, a group of veteran Democratic operatives are trading horror stories about the man in whom their party is about to invest its hopes—and those of progressives throughout America. "Did you see the picture of Kerry looking out the window of the hospital room where he was born in Denver?" asks one, as the others nod and smirk. "Yes, I have definite memories, my mother in labor, my head cresting, the light . . . the light," he says in dead-on mimicry of Kerry's sonorous cadence. "You cannot clone a personality onto someone, either they have one or they don't," says another party type. "You couldn't make up the cigarette holder and the voice for FDR, that was him." A third guy cracks up everyone with his story about a Boston supporter of Kerry's who introduced his diminutive eighty-one-year-old mother to the senator at a party function. "As they're shaking hands, he's doing what he always does, scanning the room for someone more important. So she grabs his tie and jerks him down to eye level and says, 'Hey! You look at me when I'm talking to you!'"

On the way out of a convention-opening party, the city's gleaming new convention center on the South Boston waterfront, a giant Ferris wheel has been erected—indoors!—and has attracted a line of cocktail-clutching guests, some already a bit wobbly. The gate of the Ferris wheel has a smiley face on it, but there may not be many smiley faces in evidence once the combination of the ride's motion and the booze takes its toll. For now, everyone looks happy, and one overdressed woman grabs my arm to gush about the "diversity" of the entertainment for the affair. "Isn't it wonderful that Little Richard is performing here in South Boston! I mean, after the busing and all."

Her outdated glee—South Boston has long been more integrated than most suburban communities—is in sharp contrast with the anger pouring through the car radio on a local black-community talk show as I drive home from the party. A caller is bemoaning the scarcity of black vendors hired to stage the convention by the Democratic National Committee. "It's amazing the number of African American businessmen who are willing to support the Republican Party because of that response," he says. Another caller claims he sent a letter complaining about the near "blackout" to the DNC, the convention host committee, Sen. Kerry's office, and the White House. "The only response I got was from Bush," he exclaims. "Kerry could have a problem down the road." (Coincidentally, the next day's *New York Post* carried a front-page photo of Kerry, ill advisedly posing at the mouth of the shuttle *Discovery* in a blue safety suit that makes him look like Woody Allen impersonating a sperm cell in *Everything You Always Wanted to Know about Sex.* The screaming headline: Boston, We Have a Problem.)

On the convention floor Tuesday night, Peter, Paul and Mary are struggling to warm up early arriving delegates, attracting attention only when they launch into "Blowin' in the Wind," which gets quite a few delegates up and swaying. Many of the boomers here haven't aged well. They're pasty-faced and fat. In a skybox, a Generation X anchorman is mimicking their awkward dancing. But the crowd perks up when National Education Association president Reg Weaver rises to speak, and no wonder. Nearly one-fourth of them are union members, compared with 13 percent of eligible voters nationwide. This is only one of many striking gaps between the delegates and the public at large. Half of all voters and 39 percent of all Democrats favor the death penalty; only 19 percent of the delegates agree. Only 5 percent of the Democratic delegates oppose legal recognition of same-sex couples; outside the Fleet Center, 33 percent of all Democrats and 40 percent of all voters oppose it. Three-fourths of the delegates tell pollsters abortion should be available on demand, while less than half of Democratic voters and barely a third of the general electorate agree. Accordingly, 41 percent of the delegates identify themselves as liberals, a self-description adopted by only 33 percent of Democrats and 20 percent of all voters.

Perhaps the best adjective for this crowd is "entitled." The same delegates who got out of their chairs for "Blowin' in the Wind," the 1960s anthem of righteous young boomers, slump back into them when Peter, Paul and Mary swing into "If I Had a Hammer," the left-wing call for solidarity that nearly got Pete Seeger killed by an angry anticommunist mob when he performed it in 1949. On the podium, the anti-Bush rhetoric has been toned down by order of the DNC and the Kerry campaign, which wants to "send a message the Democratic Party and Sen. Kerry are positive," explains convention chairman Bill Richardson, the governor of New Mexico. In fact, the most passionate outburst of the week comes on the convention's final night when the fire marshal orders the hall shut down due to overcrowding, locking out hundreds of bigwigs who lingered too long over the complimentary shrimp before showing up to hear Kerry's acceptance speech. A florid-faced delegate in an expensive suit and bow tie is in the hallway outside the skyboxes, bellowing for all to hear that "this is outrageous. Very important people are being shut out by this. Boston will never have another convention."

This will likely not trouble the working families who showed up as ordered four hours in advance of a James Taylor/Boston Pops concert near the Kennedy Library during convention week. The show had been billed as a gift from the party to the residents of Boston for putting up with all the hassle and lost business caused by convention security. After waiting in long lines, they were unexpectedly seated far at the back of the concert area; the seats up front had been reserved for late-arriving delegates. Said one exhausted, annoyed mother, "I guess this is the two Americas Kerry and Edwards are talking about."

Aloofness. Arrogance. Entitlement. Condescension. Hypocrisy. Memories of how those politically unappealing traits were writ large during convention week came flooding back on election night, when Ohio came in narrowly for Bush (conspiracy theories notwithstanding). The deciding factors: a weak working-class showing for Kerry and a 16 percent turnout for Bush among black voters, significantly ahead of his 11 percent black vote nationally. Boston, we have a problem, indeed. But as I write this at the end of 2006, there's cause for Democratic optimism. Bush fatigue, impatience with the war in Iraq, and disgust over congressional corruption under a Republican majority have created an opening for Democrats. Surely, now that boomer Republicans have thoroughly squandered their advantage through self-serving prosecution of a right-wing ideological agenda and obliviousness to informed dissent, boomer Democrats are in the driver's seat for 2008?

Maybe not, given the ideological hubris and groupthink that characterized the postelection fallout among Democrats. Some like Jim Wallis—the liberal minister who has been trying to get Democrats to stress their religious values—concludes that "when Democrats take a more morally sensible and centrist position on issues like abortion, they do better than liberals have done." But that sound advice must compete with the likes of lefty blogger Blue Grass Roots out of Kentucky, arguing that "half of the new Democrats entering the House could be labeled as progressives" and warning against a party move to the center. Meanwhile, from the boomer leaders of both parties comes pap. Voters want us to "work together to address the challenges facing our nation," said Bush; they are calling for a "new direction," added Nancy Pelosi. Good luck. As *Time* pointed out in a 2006 election postmortem, "barring the emergence of a Democrat who can talk about faith and appear to be centrist and progressive at the same time, Democrats will remain mired in a never-ending debate of left vs. center, Netroots vs. DLC, populist vs. business-friendly."

Nothing coming out of Washington since the election seems likely to ease the despair of Jenny Bagent, a Generation X hospital clerk in economically depressed Hopetown, Ohio, struggling to set aside college money for her two daughters. "We hope things will change, but I'm not banking on it. She told a Reuters reporter writing a postelection story from the crucial red state of 2004. "Too many of these people have never even been middle class."

Jenny would feel right at home with the beleaguered work-ing families of Massachusetts. Should she ever scratch together enough cash to finance a family vacation to a high-growth state like Nevada, Arizona, or Texas, she might well run into one of the fast-growing diaspora of Massachusetts expatriates. Consider what some of them wrote in a depressing full page of letters on reasons for leaving Massachusetts that the *Globe* ran in 2006. "We left because the American dream was no longer accessible in Massachusetts . . . [and] the concerns of ordinary citizens are so often met with disdain," wrote Joshuah Mello of Wilmington, North Carolina.

Carol McFadden, whose family ties to Massachusetts date back to 1637, was packing her bags "because of the crazy left-wing political agenda, the out-of-control cost of living, the congested can't-get-there-from-here traffic. . . . I am headed south where . . . the political climate is truly democratic."

Ed Lawrence, a corporate trainer for a high-tech company in the Boston suburbs, recounted the comments of out-of-staters who attend his classes. They say things like, 'So a few people aren't allowed to work, the state workers don't have to work, and the rest of you who have to work have to put up with it?' They would never want to live here."

Added Rita Clasby of Plympton, "Our politicians are an embarrassment, and they have demonstrated to the voters of this once-great state that 'they know better' what is good for us by the way they represent our voice.

"It wasn't the weather," agreed expat Mardy Grothe from Raleigh, North Carolina. "It was the climate."

We've fallen a long way since John Adams wrote of

Massachusetts more than two centuries ago, "The morals of our people are much better. Our manners are more polite and agreeable; our language is better, our taste better, our persons handsomer, our spirit greater, our laws wiser." With the boomers who've made a hash of things firmly in control, there is little cause to believe change is at hand. Before Deval Patrick had even taken the oath of office in early 2007, Beacon Hill was already consumed with the kind of ego-driven squabbling that boomer political culture so excels in. Top legislative Democrats were warning Patrick against encroaching on their turf, and backbenchers were complaining that his plans for an unprecedented outdoor inaugural might give them frostbite. If a dramatic reordering of their long-scrambled priorities is under consideration, it's invisible for now. The new governor's first move was to restore $425 million in spending vetoed by outgoing governor Mitt Romney after a late-session legislative feeding frenzy. Some of the funds were for justifiable social services and economic development needs, but also among the items Romney cut were a $4 million "study of the internal combustion engine," a $150,000 study of the feeding habits of the winter moth, and $100,000 earmarked for construction of a gazebo in an affluent suburb. "By restoring these cuts, [Patrick] sends the message that he will not play politics with the lives of poor and disabled people," said state Democratic Party chairman Phil Johnston, as if the poor and disabled couldn't use the funds wasted on budgetary pork.

And that wasn't the worst of it. Within six weeks of taking office, Patrick had squandered most of his political capital with a series of arrogant me-generation gaffes. His predecessor's official car was an aging Ford Crown Victoria, but Patrick, who had made a campaign promise to replace gas-guzzling state vehicles with hybrids, scrapped it in favor of a brand new Cadillac. "It's nice," he explained when reporters asked him about it. Public buzz over that choice turned ugly when it came out that the new governor, even as he prepared a budget that included cuts in social services and higher taxes, had ordered up $27,387 in fancy new furnishings for the governor's office, including $12,000 drapes and a $1,395 sideboard. Beleaguered taxpayers were furious when they learned Patrick had also hired a fundraiser from his campaign to fill a newly created $72,000 a year state job keeping the schedule of his wife Diane, a highly paid attorney for a downtown Boston law firm.

Patrick grudgingly agreed to personally cover the costs of the Caddy and the office makeover, but initially refused to back down on the patronage hire, and referred to the flak as a "hazing." He offered what seemed to be ersatz contrition a few weeks later, when he was caught making a call to a company doing business with the state on behalf of a former business crony, and a poll showed his approval rating plummeting. "What I'm not interested in, but I have to get more interested in, is government by photo-op," he told an interviewer, a breathtakingly obtuse comment from a boomer politician whose campaign amounted to one long cleverly staged photo op geared toward gullible boomers. If this is a preview of what his partner in rhetorical style, Sen. Obama, might do in office, it's daunting, to say the least.

Stories like this make all but the most sycophantic activists shake their heads in despair at the tenacity of liberal narcissism and hypocrisy in Massachusetts. But those of us who grew up here still have happier memories. As I came of age in the heart of the People's Republic, the sight of a new generation coming to power truly inspired me and my peers to dream of our state becoming an enlightened beachhead, a place where the boomer fantasy of leadership leveling the playing field and uniting the races, the genders, and the classes seemed plausible.

After everything you've read, perhaps it will surprise you to learn that I believe in abortion rights. As the father of two boys who knows what it means to see their ultrasound pictures in utero, I abhor the act; growing up and living with strong, principled women, fully capable of making decisions about their own health, I see no place for the state in their childbirth choices. I strongly support gay marriage; enjoying the company of gay friends and neighbors as I have, believing as I do that the legal and moral commitments of marriage are crucial social glue, I could never condone second-class citizenship for them. In most states, I guess I'd be considered a card-carrying liberal. So be it. I'm a boomer too, a product of the liberal idealism of my late 1960s–early 1970s adolescence.

But I'm also a liberal who's been mugged. Over twenty-five years of covering Massachusetts politics, I've seen the dream curdle into something sour and sad. When it comes to political leadership—the kind that grows with the times, responds to change, stays in close touch with the real needs and aspirations of the people it represents, and shows the rest of America how it should be done—Massachusetts, once first among equals, is now Nowheresville. Harvard Square, where I once inhaled secondhand pot smoke and political idealism in equal measure, has become a shrine to aging boomer values, a mall of national chain stores that peddle overpriced fleece and new age jewelry to the status conscious with money to burn, while the political class it has produced singles out Wal-Mart—the shopping mecca of the penny-pinching working stiff—for ridicule and attack.

The Massachusetts model has grossly failed to deliver on boomer liberalism's promises and fulfill its expectations. Democrats have limped through a generation of tenuous grasp on national political power in part because they've been infected with the Massachusetts viruses I've described: addiction to tax revenues and a raging edifice complex couched in disrespect for wage earners; phony identity politics without real results for women and minorities; reflexive anti-Americanism in foreign affairs; vain indulgence in obnoxious political correctness; self-serving featherbedding; NIMBYism; authoritarian distortion of the balance of governmental power, all simmered in a broth of hypocritical paternalism.

Cue the snappy solutions and finger-wagging bromides, right? That's the cocksure boomer formula: identify a problem, summon our historically unprecedented powers of analysis and insight, send out for sushi while we mull over the findings, and presto! Instant answers, to be quickly shoved down the throats of what we imagine to be a grateful public.

Sorry. I'm no Einstein, but I second what he said about the importance of humility: "Whoever undertakes to set himself up as a judge of Truth and Knowledge is shipwrecked by the laughter of the gods." Yet I believe in reinvention and redemption. It's the American way. The boomers may be getting on in

years, but it's not too late to honestly identify and at least try to
alter a few of the generational habits that have derailed our
youthful optimism.

Start with the lack of humility that leads boomer elites to
become dangerously isolated even as they proclaim the unique
brilliance of their listening skills. The Clintons identified the
public's desperate need to be heard early on, and have rarely
missed a chance to milk the concept. Bill held his "town meetings" during the 1992 New Hampshire primary (which a team
of Dartmouth researchers proved were mainly photo ops packed
with locals already on board with the candidate); Hillary took
her "listening tour" of the New York hinterlands during her
2000 Senate run. Cynicism aside, their political success speaks to
their willingness to actually absorb and act on some of what they
hear.

Real listening involves breaking out of ideological and social cocoons, looking beyond the usual pundits and think tanks
for policy ideas and research, monitoring Rush Limbaugh in
the car on occasion instead of NPR. More mingling with ordinary folks would help, but this can't be just the occasional
heart-to-heart with a chatty cabbie on the way to the airport, or
the artificial encounters that occur when a pol and his en-
tourage "drop by" a senior center or VFW post. Menino's
listed phone number should be standard practice for elected officials. Boomer leaders who are serious about finding out what
working people really deal with and think about might consider sinking a couple of hundred bucks into a top-notch disguise
and setting aside a couple of days a month to hang out on the
subway, in a coffee shop, anyplace where casual conversations

might be engaged in or overheard. And the information that comes from assiduous street research must take precedence over the received wisdom that saturates political elites across the spectrum. If the actions that result from guerrilla listening upset campaign donors, lobbyists, and the other usual suspects who insulate politicians from the healing properties of fresh air like a too-large bandage over a minor scrape, that's a sure sign of progress.

The most toxic aspect of the Massachusetts model is its uniformity, its relentless groupthink. The ratings success of Fox News proved how large an audience there is for an alternative to conventional wisdom; Internet sites such as www.huffing tonpost.com now provide unruly but fertile conditions for the pursuit of truly diverse discourse. Liberals who prosper politically in the future will be ones who make a point of reaching beyond the narrow circles they too often move in. It's a matter of class as well as ideology. Rev. Eugene Rivers sees a yawning gulf between the "Starbucks people" and the "Dunkin' Donuts people," a self-imposed set of defining cultural distinctions that too often prevents boomer liberals from recognizing and seizing potential common ground with voters. Contrary to the apparent belief of the likes of John Kerry, it won't kill you to eat the cheesesteak the way it's served, complete with Cheez Whiz. By consciously seeking out contrary views and suppressing the boomer instinct to assume an immutable link between personal preference and political truth, perhaps pro-tax liberals can come to understand that a $200 tax cut is no "pittance" when it means a son or daughter can pay the fee and play a varsity high-school sport. When that happens, a corner is turned toward effective leadership, and the day when that liberal's appeal for new revenue has credibility with working-class voters is closer at hand.

It is also past time to start matching liberal political policies with bedrock progressive goals. If liberals really cared about equal educational opportunity and the sorry sight of poor kids trapped in failing urban schools, they would never deny those children the opportunity to seize hope through school choice, charter schools, or even vouchers, simply because antireform teacher unions are a major source of campaign support. Yet even the Clintons never had the nerve to go too far down the road of real education reform because the unions made it clear what the consequences would be, and on cue, their liberal allies stigmatized choice as a "conservative" idea. When Judy Burnette, that Boston advocate of educational choice for low-income families, heard that Hillary Clinton had denounced a plan to give vouchers to 2,000 Washington, D.C., children from poor families as a scheme to "drain money away from the public schools," she was livid. "With all due respect, Mrs. Clinton, I would just simply ask you to look at the choice you made for your daughter," she said. (Washington's ritzy Sidwell Friends School, by the way—where else?)

What a horrific blunder. At the 1996 Democratic National Convention, I attended a reunion of the surviving members of the Chicago Seven, the radical activists who led the infamous street protests at the 1968 Chicago convention, an early boomer watershed moment. Bobby Seale, the cofounder of the Black Panther Party, told me he had given up on national politics in favor of community-based organizing that urged people to take control of their educational needs away from incompetent bureaucracies—as charter-school parents do. "The grassroots, that's where it's at," Seale said, an observation confirmed in 2006 by Deval Patrick's use of the Internet and grassroots organizing to elbow aside the hidebound Massachusetts Democratic Party.

Reclaiming the high ground in support of populist educational empowerment would be an unmistakable signal of genuine commitment to reform. The teacher unions won't like it, but where are they going to go? Any loss of donations or organizational muscle would be more than compensated for by renewed respect for liberalism among voters of all types desperate for signs of real political courage and independence, traits too often lacking from those in thrall to the Massachusetts mindset. And it would ratchet up the pressure on conservatives to show more independence from the right-wing ideologues they've pandered to. While you're at it, repeat after me: until hunger is eradicated, affordable housing needs are met, and job-killing tax burdens are reduced, no more $100,000 gazebos.

Would it be too much to ask boomer liberals to pack away political correctness in the attic alongside that box of Spirit and Iron Butterfly LPs you remember so fondly but will likely never listen to again? Liberation from the stultifying bonds of PC will free you to play political offense again, instead of chronically having to justify the demonization of parenthood, marriage, Christmas, and other bedrock symbols of American life. Your friends who cherish correctness as a mark of their own social superiority won't like it, but it's the price of admission to be respected by the baffled, angry masses who've been insulted over the years by that boomer ego trip. As Tom Frank pointed out in *What's the Matter with Kansas?* the Massachusetts-style cultural snobbery that political correctness represents may be the best thing that ever happened to the right, political manna from heaven. If the boomer liberal goal is to fill the enemy's gas tank, keep it up. If you want to win, drop the silly, arrogant affectation that PC represents.

If the Democratic rebound in Congress and the consolidation of liberal control over the bluest state show any signs of finally fulfilling boomer political destiny, we'll need a more powerful microscope to spot them. That leaves a wide-open opportunity in 2008 for power-hungry conservatives to exploit the cultural miscues, misplaced priorities, and delusional smugness of the Massachusetts model. Only a fool doubts that the right is busy reacting to its 2006 blunders, cleaning up its act, and sharpening its knives. Rudy Giuliani, John McCain, and Mitt Romney all have their baggage, most notably support for the Bush policy in Iraq. But they share underlying principles that are proven sellers at the presidential level: economic growth, robust national defense, respect for taxpayer dollars. By sheer virtue of not being Bush, they represent at least a degree of change from their party's status quo. Will boomer liberalism be ready with some changes of its own, and a candidate who can convincingly articulate them?

It had better be. The clock is ticking on America's largest generation, and its liberal wing has miles to go before it sleeps. The spiritual descendants of Kennedy country across the nation justifiably sneered as one when Bush unveiled that Mission Accomplished banner across the deck of the USS *Abraham Lincoln*.

Would there be an ounce more credibility should liberal boomers make the same claim about their own core political goals? There seems little chance that a Democratic Congress and a Republican administration that clearly loathe each other will make serious progress by November 2008 on the issues that matter to working-class Americans. The partisan blame game is already well under way. So absent a second-straight Republican meltdown, boomer Democrats must stage an intervention with themselves, hoping to break through a generation's worth of denial, conceit, and obsession. Will they heed the barking of Blue Dog Democrats, whose ranks include some of the breakthrough winners of 2006 and defuse the Republican edge on cultural issues by talking to voters about abortion and gay rights in less dogmatic terms? Will they allay the fears of the financially stressed by modeling fiscal restraint and a commitment to positive economic growth? Will they tone down the grandiosity, turn off the PC jargon, and tune in to what skeptical constituents really want—and don't want—from them? Can they avoid the toxic instinct to always blame America first, while considering the flaws in their own arguments last?

In other words, are they ready to finally grow up, see the worn-out nostrums of Kennedy country for the dead end they are, and take a different route? After all, before you can fix what's the matter with Kansas, you have to repair what's wrong with Massachusetts.

INDEX